A Primer on SQL

The Times Mirror/Mosby Data Processing and Information Systems Series

A PRIMER ON SQL

ROY AGELOFF

University of Rhode Island

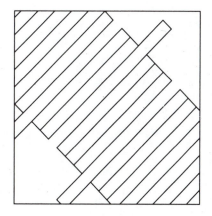

IRWIN

Homewood, IL 60401
Boston, MA 02116

To Hilda, with love.

Editor
Susan A. Solomon

Production Coordinator
House of Graphics, Mountain View, California

Text and Cover Designer
Joe di Chiarro

Copyeditor
Betty Drury

FIRST EDITION

Copyright © 1988 by Times Mirror/Mosby College Publishing
A division of The C.V. Mosby Company
11830 Westline Industrial Drive, St. Louis, MO 63146

Printed in the United States of America

Library of Congress Cataloging-in-Publication Data

Ageloff, Roy, 1943–
    A primer on SQL.

    Includes index.
    1. SQL (Computer program language)   2. Data base management.
I. Title.
QA76.73.S67A34   1988   005.75'65   87-30200
ISBN 0-8016-0085-5

HOG/VH/VH   9 8 7 6 5   02/B/275

Preface

WHY THIS TEXT IS NEEDED

SQL continues to gain acceptance as the database language of choice. Yet, to date, almost all of the text material on SQL can be found only within chapters or parts of chapters of database management textbooks. A text dedicated to a first course on SQL is needed. It should be flexible enough that it can be used in a variety of instructional settings. Further, it should provide simple explanations of SQL commands and numerous, easy-to-understand examples suitable for first-time SQL users. The promise of this text is that it will meet all of these needs.

AUDIENCE

Except for the last chapter (Chapter 10 on Embedded SQL), this text assumes no prior computer programming experience.

In a college or university setting, this book can be used as a supplement in a Principles of Database course or in other courses such as End-User Computing, Fourth-Generation Languages, and Decision Support Systems. For those introductory computer courses that include a language segment, *A Primer on SQL* could replace or serve as a complement to a procedural language such as BASIC.

End users in industry and government who are currently using or planning to use SQL will find *A Primer on SQL* an appropriate primary text for their workshops, seminars, and other training programs.

REASONS TO USE THIS BOOK

A Primer on SQL offers comprehensive pedagogy:

Coverage

The emphasis of this text is on careful treatment of the essential syntax of SQL. The end user does not need to know every aspect of SQL but will want to be comfortable with the essentials of the language. Thus, this text stresses the basics over completeness. At the same time, it includes topics that receive little or no coverage in database management texts, such as system catalog commands, formatting queries, saving and retrieving queries, use of parameters in queries, and embedded SQL.

Presentation

Topics are presented with marked attention to the explanation of how each statement works. Boxed topics, program notes, and other text design features are used to set off key material such as the syntax of commands. All key terms are boldfaced on their first mention.

Case Examples

A realistic and familiar Case Example is used throughout the text in an effort to make queries meaningful. In addition, complete queries and results are presented based upon this Case Example.

Exercises

This text includes a carefully designed set of exercises called *Your Turn*. These exercises are strategically placed after the thorough presentation of important topics. Each exercise is designed to reinforce, integrate, or extend the preceding topic. The answers to the *Your Turn* exercises are included at the back of the text.

Also at the end of each chapter, you will find the *Video Rental, Inc. Case Chapter Assignment*. This has been included to provide a new Case Example for additional practice and concept reinforcement.

Software and Coupon Savings

Actual hands-on use of SQL is provided free to adopters of this text. Times Mirror/Mosby is pleased to offer adopters free of charge XDB-STUDENT, a two-diskette limited-use version of XDB-SQL, a DB2-compatible package published by Software Systems Technology. This software will allow up to 30 records per table and will run on the IBM PC and compatibles. A User Manual compiled by Roy Ageloff is available with the software. Contact your Times Mirror/Mosby representative for details.

Also in cooperation with Software Systems Technology, Times Mirror/ Mosby has included at the end of this text a coupon for a $100.00 savings on the purchase of the full commercial version of XDB-SQL.

HOW TO USE THIS BOOK

Chapters 2 through 6 are aimed at the end user, as they cover the essentials of interactive SQL. Chapters 7 through 10 will benefit programmers, systems analysts, database administrators, and others with similar backgrounds. These chapters deal with some of the administrative aspects of SQL.

Some of the material in the text may be too technical for end users. These portions of the text are identified by triple asterisks (***) and can be skipped without loss of continuity. Further, material on formatting (Appendix A) can be introduced any time after Chapter 3. The *Video Rental, Inc.* Case Example can be assigned immediately and serve as another set of exercises. The examples within the text, the *Your Turn* exercises, and the *Video Rental, Inc.* Case Example assignments can all be completed using XDB-STUDENT, which is provided with this text.

OF RELATED INTEREST

Database Systems for Management

Written by James Courtney and David Paradice, this core database text is designed to support a management-oriented first course on database concepts. It features

- A managerial orientation, emphasizing decision making and the impact of the database environment on the decision-making process.

- Case Examples, which provide relevant business scenarios.

- The User's View, which addresses the special managerial issues specific to database users.

- Municipal Authority of Lincoln, which is a comprehensive, ongoing case study.

Cases in Database Design

Traditionally, publishers have failed to provide good case material to supplement database textbooks. Students need practical, realistic business cases to reinforce the database concepts taught, particularly in the management-oriented course. Written by Ludwig Slusky, this 200-page casebook provides flexibility to allow individual or team experience with database design fundamentals. It contains

- Five industry-oriented cases on database design based on manufacturing, financial, and marketing applications and supported by practical guidelines and explanations.

- Assignments with multivalued requirements for data relationships, so the instructor can assign the same project over several terms with varying solutions and results.

- Blank forms for all the cases.

ACKNOWLEDGMENTS

I thank the reviewers of this text for their valuable suggestions and their commitment to the reviewing schedule.

Norman Brammer
Colorado State University

Larry Cornwall
Bradley University

John Crawford
California Polytechnic Institute,
San Louis Obispo

Ralph Duffy
Northern Seattle Community College

Henry Etlinger
Rochester Institute of Technology

Allen P. Gray
Loyola Marymount University

Jan Harrington
Bentley College

Susan Lenker
Central Michigan University

Richard G. Ramirez
Arizona State University

John Shepherd
Duquense University

Glenn Smith
James Madison University

Further, I wish to thank Mike Provost at IBM for providing me with valuable reference materials.

Many thanks to the University of Rhode Island's Computer Science Computer Laboratory staff for allowing me to use their facilities. To Bobbi Rothstein and Stu Westin, two colleagues at the University of Rhode Island, thanks for your many helpful suggestions concerning the manuscript.

Thanks to the production team for their effort. In particular, I wish to thank Joe di Chiarro, Betty Drury, and Alex Teshin and Chris Kantoff at House of Graphics for their hard work.

My deep appreciation to Susan Solomon, Editor, whose foresight made this project a reality.

And finally, to Hilda, my sounding board, friend, and number one supporter, I dedicate this book.

Roy Ageloff

Contents in Brief

Contents in Detail

Chapter 1

Introduction

The repository of information within an organization is the **database**. It is the foundation upon which computer applications are developed. A database is defined by James Martin as "a shared collection of interrelated data designed to meet the needs of multiple types of end users....The objective of database technology is to speed up computer application development, reduce application maintenance cost, and provide end users with the data they need for doing their jobs as efficiently as possible." (*An End-User's Guide to Data Base* [Englewood Cliffs, N.J.: Prentice-Hall, 1981], p. v.)

In order to build or manage a database, a software system is needed to integrate the data and provide different views of the database to different users. A **database management system (DBMS)** is the software that makes it possible to access integrated data within a database environment.

The DBMS works as an "intermediary" in the database environment. It serves as an interface between the database and the people seeking data from the database. The function of the DBMS is to provide an environment where it is convenient and efficient to retrieve information from and store data in the database. Specifically, the DBMS provides for the definition of the database and for data storage. It offers a mechanism through which users access and manipulate data. Through security, backup and recovery, and other services, the DBMS protects the stored data.

Most DBMSs structure the database on one of three data models: hierarchical, network, or relational. In this text, we will be concerned only with the relational data model.

RELATIONAL DATABASES

Most recent DBMSs are based on the relational data model. The fundamental organizational structure for data in the relational model is the relation. A **relation** is a two-dimensional table made up of rows and columns. Each relation, or table as it is often called, stores data about **entities.** These entities are objects or events on which an organization chooses to collect data. Customers, employees, products, and bank accounts are examples of entities. The columns in a relation represent characteristics (**attributes**, **fields**, or **data items**) of an entity, such as employee number, employee name, address, etc. The rows (called **tuples** in relational jargon) in the relation represent specific occurrences (or records) of a customer, employee, bank account, product, etc. Each row consists of a sequence of values, one for each column in the table. In addition, each row (or record) in a table must be unique. The **primary key** of a relation is the attribute or attributes whose value uniquely identifies a specific row in a relation. For example, an employee identification number (ID) is normally used as a primary key for employee records.

Over the years, many different sets of terms have been used interchangeably when discussing the relational model. Table 1.1 lists these terms and shows their relationship.

TABLE 1.1	Relational Database Terminology		
	Relational Model Literature	**Relational DBMS Products**	**File Processing**
	Relation	Table	File
	Tuple	Row	Record
	Attribute	Column	Field

Figure 1.1 illustrates two relations. The first one depicts customers and the second represents outstanding customer invoices. A row in the CUSTOMER relation represents a particular customer, while a row in the INVOICE relation represents a customer invoice. Thus, a relation provides a structure for storing data about some entity within the organization. In fact, a database in the relational model consists of several relations, each representing a different entity.

An important characteristic of the relational model is that records stored in one table can be related to records stored in other tables by matching common data values from the different tables. Thus, data in different relations can be tied together, or integrated. For example, in Figure 1.1, invoice 71115 in the INVOICE relation is related to customer 112, FRAZIER, in the CUSTOMER relation because they both have the same customer ID. Invoices 71119, 71123, and 71125 are also related to customer 112.

A database in the relational model is made up of a collection of interrelated relations. Each relation represents data (to the users of the database) as a two-dimensional table. The terms *relation* and *table* are interchangeable. For the remainder of the text, the term *table* will be used when referring to a relation.

Access to data in the database is accomplished in two ways. The first way is by writing application programs in procedural languages such as COBOL, FORTRAN, and PL/I that add, modify, delete, and retrieve data from the database. These functions are performed by issuing requests to the DBMS. The second method of accessing data is accomplished by issuing commands, or **queries**, in a fourth-generation language (4GL) directly to the DBMS to find certain data. This

FIGURE 1.1 CUSTOMER and INVOICE Relations

a. CUSTOMER Relation

CUSTOMER ID	CUSTOMER NAME	ADDRESS	CITY	STATE
107	PRYOR	1 NINIGRET AV	QUONSETT	RI
111	MARGOLIS	3 CHESTER AV	WESTERLY	RI
112	FRAZIER	7 CONCH RD	NEW LONDON	CT
123	CHEN	163 NAMCOCK RD	ATTLEBORO	MA
128	STECKERT	14 HOMESTEAD	NORWICH	CT

b. INVOICE Relation

INVOICE NUMBER	DATE	AMOUNT	CUSTOMER ID
71115	12/14/87	55.20	112
71116	12/14/87	121.25	123
71118	12/16/87	23.95	111
71119	12/16/87	54.50	112
71120	12/16/87	88.00	107
71121	12/16/87	45.40	111
71123	12/17/87	18.75	112
71124	12/17/87	33.80	128
71125	12/17/87	39.50	112

language is called a **query language**, which is a nonprocedural language characterized by high-level English-like commands such as UPDATE, DELETE, SELECT, etc. Structured Query Language (SQL) is an example of a nonprocedural query language.

EVOLUTION OF SQL

Relational database management systems evolved from an underlying theoretical framework known as the relational model. The underlying theory was developed by E. F. Codd while working at the IBM Systems Research Lab. This work was based on mathematical principles, specifically on set theory and relational calculus. The research, first published in 1970, eventually led to a prototype version of the relational model using SQL (sometimes pronounced "sequel"). This system was known as SYSTEM R. One of the initial drawbacks of this system was that it was too slow to handle large commercial databases. As relational technology improved, the performance issue became less important. In the early 1980s, IBM released two commercial products based on the relational model: SQL/DS and DATABASE2 (DB2). Both products are similar but work on different IBM operating systems.

As more corporate data processing centers use SQL, more vendors, such as ORACLE, are offering relational database products based on the SQL language. Table 1.2 shows a partial list of vendors who currently support the SQL language.

TABLE 1.2	SQL Vendors and Products	
Vendor	**Product**	**Computer Type**
Cincom	SUPRA	Mainframe/Mini
Gupta Technology	SQLBASE	Micro
Informix Software	INFORMIX/SQL	Mini/Micro
IBM	Database2 (DB2)	Mainframe
IBM	SQL/DS	Mainframe
Oracle Corporation	ORACLE	Mainframe/Mini/Micro
Relational Technology	INGRES	Mini/Micro
Software Systems Technology	XDB	Micro

In 1986, the American National Standards Institute (ANSI) approved SQL as the standard relational database language. SQL is now emerging as the standard query language for relational database management systems.

The purpose of this text is to explain SQL so that users of this language will be able to write queries accessing data from a database.

CASE EXAMPLE: BACKGROUND INFORMATION FOR THE INTEGRATED STUDENT RECORD SYSTEM

To provide a frame of reference to show the concepts and syntax of SQL, we will use an integrated Student Record System for a typical university throughout the text.

A university's Student Record System is a complex database application, far more complex than this brief description indicates. However, the Student Record System you use will be simplified so that the complexity of the application does not interfere with the purpose of this text: to introduce you to the database language SQL.

An integrated Student Record System involves many departments within a university. The major departments include Admissions, Registrar, Bursar, Financial Aid, Housing and Dining Services, Health Services, and Academic.

Various users in these departments require information to help them carry out their functions. Thus, they will need a number of reports, such as the following:

- Student listings
- Mailing labels
- Student course schedules
- Student transcripts
- Student grade reports
- Class rosters at beginning of and during term

- Graded roster at end of term
- Grade profile study
- Dean's list report
- Academic actions
- Enrollment summaries
    by major
    by level
    by sex
- Other relevant reports

In addition, these users need online access to the Student Record System to aid them in performing their duties. Some of the queries are known in advance, or are preplanned; for example:

- Information on a given student
    name, address, phone
    current term's schedule
- Information on a given course
    where offered
    who is teaching
- Information on a given faculty member
- Other relevant queries

Other queries are unplanned, or ad-hoc. The system must have the capability to answer these unplanned, one-time-only queries in addition to the preplanned queries.

All of the daily activities of a university create a need for recording and storing vast amounts of data. These activities affect the Student Record System in numerous ways. Here is a partial list of actions or events that impact the Student Record System. Data concerning these transactions must be captured in order to keep the data in the system accurate.

- Students
    are admitted, leave, graduate.
    choose majors, change majors.
    apply for housing.
    pay tuition and fees.
    add courses, drop courses, complete courses.
- Faculty
    are hired, leave, promoted.
    given salary increases.
    assign grades, change grades.
- Other relevant activities

Remember, we mentioned that a university's Student Record System is a complex database application. For our purposes, however, the database will consist of four tables, as follows:

a. STUDENT Table   Each row represents data about a student in the university.

b. FACULTY Table   Each row represents data about a faculty member employed by the university.

c. COURSE Table   Each row represents a course being taught during the current term.

d. CRSENRL Table   Each row represents a student course registration. For example, if a student is enrolled in three courses, three rows would appear in this table.

Figure 1.2 shows the layout of each of the four tables. The sample data stored in each table appears in Figure 1.3.

FIGURE 1.2   Description of Student Record System Tables

a. STUDENT Table

Column Description	Column Name	Data Type	Length	Decimal Places	Nulls Allowed*	Codes
Student ID number	SID	Character	3		No	
Student name	SNAME	Character	10		No	
Gender	SEX	Character	1		Yes	F or M
Program of study	MAJOR	Character	3		Yes	ACC FIN MGT MKT
Grade point average	GPA	Decimal	3	2	Yes	

b. FACULTY Table

Column Description	Column Name	Data Type	Length	Decimal Places	Nulls Allowed*	Codes
Faculty ID number	FID	Character	3		No	
Faculty last name	FNAME	Character	10		No	
Phone extension	EXT	Character	3		Yes	
Department	DEPT	Character	3		Yes	ACC FIN MGT MKT
Rank of faculty	RANK	Character	4		Yes	INST ASST ASSO FULL
Salary	SALARY	Integer			Yes	

(continued on next page)

c. COURSE Table

Column Description	Column Name	Data Type	Length	Decimal Places	Nulls Allowed*	Codes
Course number	CRSNBR	Character	6		No	
Course title	CNAME	Character	20		No	
Number of credits	CREDIT	Character	1		Yes	
Maximum number allowed	MAXENRL	Small integer			Yes	
Faculty ID of person teaching course	FID	Character	3		Yes	

d. CRSENRL Table

Column Description	Column Name	Data Type	Length	Decimal Places	Nulls Allowed*	Codes
Course number	CRSNBR	Character	6		No	
Student ID number	SID	Character	3		No	
Grade for course	GRADE	Character	1		Yes	

*Nulls Allowed means a record can be stored in this table if the value for this column is unknown.

FIGURE 1.3　　Sample Data for Student Record System Tables

a. STUDENT Table

SID	SNAME	SEX	MAJOR	GPA
987	POIRIER	F	MGT	3.2
763	PARKER	F	FIN	2.7
218	RICHARDS	M	ACC	2.4
359	PELNICK	F	FIN	3.6
862	FAGIN	M	MGT	2.2
748	MEGLIN	M	MGT	2.8
506	LEE	M	FIN	2.7
581	GAMBRELL	F	MKT	3.8
372	QUICK	F	MGT	3.5
126	ANDERSON	M	ACC	3.7

b. FACULTY Table

FID	FNAME	EXT	DEPT	RANK	SALARY
036	BARGES	325	MGT	ASSO	35000
117	JARDIN	212	FIN	FULL	33000
098	KENNEDY	176	ACC	ASSO	30000
075	SAMPLE	171	MKT	ASST	25000
138	WARD	125	MGT	INST	20000
219	PETERS	220	FIN	FULL	45000
151	DARDEN	250	ACC	ASSO	37000
113	PIERCE	205	MGT	INST	22000

(continued on next page)

c. COURSE Table

CRSNBR	CNAME	CREDIT	MAXENRL	FID
MGT630	INTRO TO MANAGEMENT	4	30	138
FIN601	MANAGERIAL FINANCE	4	25	117
MKT610	MKTING FOR MANAGERS	3	35	075
ACC661	TAXATION	3	30	098
FIN602	INVESTMENT SKILLS	3	25	219
ACC610	BASIC ACCOUNTING	4	25	098
MGT681	INTERNATIONAL MGT	3	20	036
MKT670	PRODUCT MARKETING	3	20	075

d. CRSENRL Table

CRSNBR	SID	GRADE
MGT630	987	A
FIN602	987	B
MKT610	987	A
FIN601	763	B
FIN602	763	B
ACC610	763	B
ACC610	218	A
ACC661	218	A
MGT630	218	C
MGT630	359	F
MGT681	359	B
MKT610	359	A
MKT610	862	A
MKT670	862	A
ACC610	862	B
MGT630	748	C
MGT681	748	B
FIN601	748	A

This chapter has introduced you to several concepts and terms related to relational database management systems. In addition, you were provided with the background information for the integrated Student Record System case that will be used throughout the text. In the next chapter, you will learn how to define and remove tables in SQL.

Chapter 2

Table Definition

SQL is a database language that permits users to define, access, and manipulate data stored in a database. This chapter describes how a table is defined and deleted. In addition, you will be shown an example of how data is loaded into a table.

CREATING THE STUDENT TABLE

One of the tables in the Student Record System case is the STUDENT table. This table is created in SQL by issuing the CREATE TABLE command.

If you enter

```
CREATE TABLE   STUDENT
     ( SID         CHAR(3)  NOT NULL,
       SNAME       CHAR(10),
       SEX         CHAR(1),
       MAJOR       CHAR(3),
       GPA         DECIMAL(3,2) )
```

SQL statements can be entered on one or more lines. Indenting is recommended to improve readability, but it is not required.

the message on the screen will be

Table Created

When the table is created, the computer displays this message.

The CREATE TABLE command is entered interactively at a terminal. Note that the list of column definitions is enclosed in parentheses and that each column definition is separated from the next column definition by a comma. In all examples in this text, each SQL statement is shown in uppercase letters to help you identify what is to be entered at the terminal. However, you actually can enter the statement in either upper- or lowercase.

The first line in the CREATE TABLE statement identifies the name of the table: STUDENT. The next five lines define the five columns that make up the STUDENT table.

1. The first column, named SID, stores the student's ID. Since NOT NULL has been included in the definition, data for a student whose ID is unknown will not be stored in the STUDENT table even if other student data (name, sex, major) is known.

2. The second column, named SNAME, stores the student's name. No name longer than ten characters can be stored in this column.

3. The third column, named SEX, contains a one-character code: F for female and M for male.

4. The fourth column, named MAJOR, stores the student's major. We will use a three-character code to represent the following majors:

   ACC for Accounting
   FIN for Finance
   MKT for Marketing
   MGT for Management

5. The fifth column, named GPA, stores the student's grade point average. A number between 0 and 9, including fractional parts to two decimal places, can be stored. However, we will only store real values between 0 and 4, which represent the valid range for a GPA in this institution.

Tables defined with the CREATE TABLE command are referred to as **base tables**. The table definition is automatically stored in a data dictionary referred to as the **system catalog**. This catalog is made up of various tables that store descriptive and statistical information related to the database. The catalog can be accessed to retrieve information about the contents and structure of the database. The system catalog is discussed in more detail in Chapter 9.

As shown in Figure 2.1, the CREATE TABLE command results in an empty table.

FIGURE 2.1   STUDENT Table after the CREATE TABLE Command

STUDENT Table

SID	SNAME	SEX	MAJOR	GPA

No data is stored in the table at the time it is created.

INSERTING DATA INTO THE STUDENT TABLE

Once the table has been created, and before any data can be retrieved, data must be added to the table using the INSERT command. The first row is added to the STUDENT table as follows:

If you enter

Columns defined as character (CHAR) have values enclosed in single quotes.

```
INSERT INTO STUDENT
VALUES ('987','POIRIER','F','MGT',3.2)
```

Parentheses must be placed around the set of data values. Each data value is separated by a comma.

the message displayed on the screen will be

```
1 Record Created
```

In the above statement, one row of data was stored in the STUDENT table. Figure 2.2 shows the STUDENT table after the first record has been added.

FIGURE 2.2   STUDENT Table with One Row Inserted

STUDENT Table

SID	SNAME	SEX	MAJOR	GPA
987	POIRIER	F	MGT	3.2

To add the second row into the STUDENT table, you enter the INSERT command again.

If you enter

```
INSERT INTO STUDENT
VALUES ('763','PARKER','F','FIN',2.7)
```

the message displayed on the screen will be

```
1 Record Created
```

Figure 2.3 shows the contents of the STUDENT table after two rows have been added.

FIGURE 2.3   STUDENT Table with Two Rows Inserted

STUDENT Table

SID	SNAME	SEX	MAJOR	GPA
987	POIRIER	F	MGT	3.2
763	PARKER	F	FIN	2.7

Additional INSERT commands are used to enter the student data illustrated in Figure 2.4. A more complete description of the INSERT command appears in Chapter 6.

FIGURE 2.4   STUDENT Table with All Data Inserted

STUDENT Table

SID	SNAME	SEX	MAJOR	GPA
987	POIRIER	F	MGT	3.2
763	PARKER	F	FIN	2.7
218	RICHARDS	M	ACC	2.4
359	PELNICK	F	FIN	3.6
862	FAGIN	M	MGT	2.2
748	MEGLIN	M	MGT	2.8
506	LEE	M	FIN	2.7
581	GAMBRELL	F	MKT	3.8
372	QUICK	F	MGT	3.5
126	ANDERSON	M	ACC	3.7

DEFINING A TABLE

As illustrated in the creation of the STUDENT table, tables are created in SQL when you specify their structure and characteristics by executing a CREATE TABLE command. The form of this command is

```
CREATE TABLE    table-name
    ( column-name1 data-type  [NOT NULL]
      [, column-name2 data-type  [NOT NULL] ] ...)
```

An SQL statement may contain optional clauses or keywords. These optional parts are included in the statement only if needed. Any clause within brackets indicates an optional clause.

COMMAND DISCUSSION

The CREATE TABLE command gives the name of the table, the name of each column in the table, and the type of data placed in each column. It can also indicate whether null values are permitted in columns.

Table Names

Each table in SQL is assigned a name. On many SQL implementations, a table name can have up to 18 characters. The first character must be a letter, but the remaining characters can include numbers, letters, and the underscore (_) character. For example, STUDENT, FACULTY and CRS_ENRL are all valid table names.

Column Names

A column stores data on one attribute. In our example, we have attributes such as student ID, major, and grade point average. Each column within a table has a unique name and may consist of up to 18 characters. On many SQL implementations, the first character must be a letter and the remaining characters may consist of letters, numbers, and the underscore. No blank spaces are allowed in the column name. Table 2.1 shows examples of valid and invalid column names.

TABLE 2.1   Valid and Invalid Column Names

Valid Column Names	Invalid Column Names	Reason Invalid
EMPNBR	EMP-NBR	Hyphen is not allowed.
EMP_NBR	EMP.NBR	Period is not allowed.
COST1	COST_IN_$	$ is not allowed.
COST_PER_MILE	COST PER MILE	Spaces are not allowed.
SALES1987	1987SALES	Name cannot start with a number.

Data Types

Each column within a table can store only one type of data. For example, a column of names represents character data, a column storing units sold represents integer data, and a column of grade point averages represents decimal data. In SQL, each column name defined in the CREATE TABLE statement has a data type declared with it. These data types include integer, decimal, and character. In addition, many versions of SQL support a Date data type. Table 2.2 illustrates the general format for each data type.

TABLE 2.2	Data Types Used in SQL				
	Type of Data	**SQL Syntax**	**Description**	**SQL Example**	**Data Value**
	Character	CHAR(length)	Used to store character data, such as names, job titles, addresses, etc. Length represents the maximum number of characters that can be stored in this column.	CHAR(25)	SMITH 10 Newman Rd
	Numeric	DECIMAL(p,s)	Used to store numbers with a fractional part, such as GPA, hourly rate, cost per unit, etc. The "p" represents the number of digits in the number and "s" represents the digits to the right of the decimal.	DECIMAL(7,2)	87.35 –4247.108
	Numeric	FLOAT	Used to store real numbers where numerical precision is important. Very large or very small numbers expressed in scientific notation (E notation).	FLOAT	8.413E-04
	Numeric	INTEGER	Used to store large whole numbers; i.e., those without a fractional part, such as population, units sold, sales in dollars. The largest integer value is +2147483647. The smallest integer value is –2147483648.	INTEGER	657899932
	Numeric	SMALLINT	Used to store small whole numbers that require few digits; for example, age,	SMALLINT	19 –432

(continued on next page)

weight, temperature.
The largest value is
+32767. The smallest
value is −32768.

Date	DATE	Used to store dates. The format is day, month, year, represented as DD-MON-YY or MM/DD/YYYY.	DATE	25–JUL–87 7/25/1987

NOT NULL Keyword

In the definition of a column, the NOT NULL keyword is optional. If a NOT NULL keyword is specified, the column may not contain a null, or unknown, value. Any attempt to place a null value in such a column is rejected. For example, assume the NOT NULL keyword is part of the definition of student ID, a column in the STUDENT table. In this case, if you tried to add a student that didn't include a student ID, you would not be able to add the record to the table.

If NOT NULL is omitted from a column definition, then a NULL value can be assigned to that column if the value is unknown. For example, assume the definition of the student name, sex, major, and grade point average columns does not include the NOT NULL keyword. Then, even though a student's grade point average is not known (or name, sex, or major, for that matter), the student's record can be added to the table. In the case of the student's grade point average, a null value is assigned.

The order in which the columns are listed in the CREATE TABLE command is the order in which the column names will appear in the table.

EXAMPLE 2.1   Based on the information in Figure 1.2b, the FACULTY table is created.

If you enter

```
CREATE TABLE  FACULTY
   ( FID      CHAR(3)    NOT NULL,
     FNAME    CHAR(10)   NOT NULL,
     EXT      CHAR(3),
     DEPT     CHAR(3),
     RANK     CHAR(4),
     SALARY   INTEGER )
```

(continued on next page)

the message displayed on the screen will be

Table Created

Since NOT NULL has been included in the definition of faculty ID and name, a faculty record without either an ID or a name will not be inserted into the FACULTY table.

Figure 2.5 shows the FACULTY table after the CREATE TABLE command has been issued.

FIGURE 2.5   FACULTY Table

FACULTY Table

FID	FNAME	EXT	DEPT	RANK	SALARY

YOUR TURN

Sections entitled *Your Turn* appear throughout the text after important topics are covered. These exercises are designed to reinforce your understanding of the preceding material. Answers to these exercises are found in Appendix E.

1. Redo the CREATE TABLE command on page 9 to reflect each of the following situations:

   a. A name field large enough to store first and last names. A length of 25 characters should suffice.

   b. Include a separate column for the first name (FIRST_NAME), 10 characters in length, and another column for the last name (LAST_NAME), 15 characters in length.

   c. Both the student ID and name must be known before a student record is stored.

   d. Include a column for combined SAT score (integer value between 400 and 1600).

   e. Include a column for a student's date of birth.

2. Use the information in Figure 1.2c to create the COURSE table.

3. Use the information in Figure 1.2d to create the CRSENRL table.

REMOVING A TABLE

When a table is no longer needed, it is deleted with the DROP TABLE command. The format of this command is

```
DROP TABLE   table-name
```

COMMAND DISCUSSION

The information about the indicated table is removed from the system catalog tables that SQL maintains on all tables in the database. In effect, you can no longer access, add, modify, or delete data stored in the table. From the user's viewpoint, the table definition and the data stored in the table have been eliminated.

EXAMPLE 2.2   The STUDENT table is no longer needed. Delete this table.

If you enter

```
DROP TABLE   STUDENT
```

the message displayed on the screen will be

```
Table Dropped
```

YOUR TURN   **4.** The FACULTY table is no longer needed. Delete this table.

This chapter has covered the creation and dropping of SQL tables. You were also shown how to insert data into a table. In the next chapter, you will learn how to query the database, an important feature of SQL.

Video Rental, Inc. Case
CHAPTER ASSIGNMENT

Read the background material for the Video Rental, Inc. case in Appendix C. Then do the following:

1. Create the MEMBER table.
2. Create the MOVIE table.
3. Create the RENTHEAD table
4. Create the RENTDETL table.

Chapter 3

Queries—A First Look

SQL is a query language that gives users access to data stored in a relational database. The data manipulation component of this language enables a user to

- write queries to retrieve information from the database.
- modify existing data in the database.
- add new data to the database.
- delete data from the database.

In Chapter 3 and the following two chapters, we will review the query capabilities of SQL. In Chapter 6, we will study the update, add, and delete features of the language.

After the tables have been created and loaded with data, you can answer requests for information from a database without the help of professional programmers. You write a question, also called a query, that consists of a single statement explaining what the user wants to accomplish. Based on this query, the computer retrieves the results and displays them at your terminal. In this chapter, you will study some of the simpler ways to form queries.

In SQL, you retrieve data from tables using the SELECT statement, which consists of one or more SELECT-FROM-WHERE blocks. The structure of this statement, in its simplest form, consists of one block containing three clauses: SELECT, FROM, and WHERE. The form of this statement is

```
SELECT    column-name1 [, column-name2] ...
FROM      table-name
[WHERE    search-condition]
```

... Indicates additional column names can be added.

Brackets surrounding a clause means the clause is optional.

COMMAND DISCUSSION

1. The SELECT clause lists the column names that you want displayed in answer to the query.

2. The FROM clause indicates the table of data "FROM" which you want to retrieve information.

3. The WHERE clause is used to screen the rows you want to retrieve, based on some criteria, or search condition, that you specify. This clause is optional, and, if omitted, all rows from the table are retrieved.

RETRIEVING FROM THE ENTIRE TABLE

To retrieve the columns you want displayed, indicate the column names after the keyword SELECT. The order in which the column names appear after the SELECT clause is the order in which these columns will be displayed.

EXAMPLE 3.1   Let's retrieve a list of all students.

If you enter the SQL statement

```
SELECT   SNAME
FROM     STUDENT
```

the result displayed on the screen will be

SNAME ─────────────────────────────── **The column name is automatically used as the column heading.**

POIRIER
PARKER
RICHARDS
PELNICK
FAGIN
MEGLIN
LEE
GAMBRELL
QUICK
ANDERSON

The first line in the SELECT statement indicates the column name SNAME is to be displayed. The second line indicates that SNAME is found in the STUDENT table.

EXAMPLE 3.2   If you want to display student names, majors, and grade point averages, you must specify that information in the SELECT clause.

If you enter the SQL statement

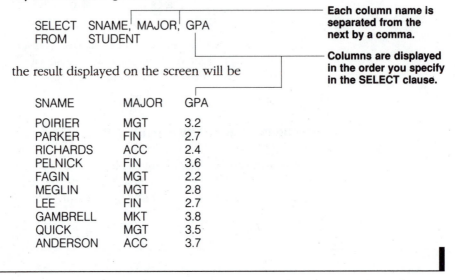

```
SELECT   SNAME, MAJOR, GPA
FROM     STUDENT
```

Each column name is separated from the next by a comma.

the result displayed on the screen will be

Columns are displayed in the order you specify in the SELECT clause.

SNAME	MAJOR	GPA
POIRIER	MGT	3.2
PARKER	FIN	2.7
RICHARDS	ACC	2.4
PELNICK	FIN	3.6
FAGIN	MGT	2.2
MEGLIN	MGT	2.8
LEE	FIN	2.7
GAMBRELL	MKT	3.8
QUICK	MGT	3.5
ANDERSON	ACC	3.7

Retrieving All the Columns

You don't need to know the column names to select data from a table. By placing an asterisk (*) in the SELECT clause, all columns of the table identified in the FROM clause will be displayed. This is an alternative to listing all the column names in the SELECT clause.

EXAMPLE 3.3   Let's look at all the data stored in the STUDENT table.

If you enter the statement

```
SELECT   *
FROM     STUDENT
```

the result displayed on the screen will be

SID	SNAME	SEX	MAJOR	GPA
987	POIRIER	F	MGT	3.2
763	PARKER	F	FIN	2.7
218	RICHARDS	M	ACC	2.4

(continued on next page)

359	PELNICK	F	FIN	3.6
862	FAGIN	M	MGT	2.2
748	MEGLIN	M	MGT	2.8
506	LEE	M	FIN	2.7
581	GAMBRELL	F	MKT	3.8
372	QUICK	F	MGT	3.5
126	ANDERSON	M	ACC	3.7

Removing Duplicate Rows

The results of a query may include duplicate rows. Sometimes the duplicates do not provide you with the precise answer you want, so you may want to eliminate them.

The use of the qualifier DISTINCT in the SELECT clause eliminates duplicate rows. As a result, the row is displayed only once.

EXAMPLE 3.4   What are the different majors offered at the university?

Version A:

Version B:

If you enter

If you enter

```
SELECT  MAJOR
FROM    STUDENT
```

```
SELECT  DISTINCT MAJOR
FROM    STUDENT
```

the result displayed
on the screen will be

the result displayed
on the screen will be

MAJOR

MAJOR

MGT
FIN
ACC
FIN
MGT
MGT
FIN
MKT
MGT
ACC

MGT ———————————— **Notice that the repeti-**
FIN   **tion of majors is elimi-**
ACC   **nated by using the**
MKT   **qualifier DISTINCT.**

(continued on next page)

Compare the results of the two versions. When DISTINCT is omitted (Version A), the major of each student is displayed; thus, the results include several duplicate rows. However, when DISTINCT is included (Version B), no duplicate major codes are displayed.

When you use DISTINCT, however, the entire row being displayed must be unique. Otherwise, the row is not considered identical, and it will not be removed. For example:

If you enter the SQL statement

```
SELECT   DISTINCT MAJOR, SNAME
FROM     STUDENT
```

the result displayed on the screen will be

MAJOR	SNAME
MGT	POIRIER
FIN	PARKER
ACC	RICHARDS
FIN	PELNICK
MGT	FAGIN
MGT	MEGLIN
FIN	LEE
MKT	GAMBRELL
MGT	QUICK
ACC	ANDERSON

In this query, duplicate major codes are displayed, since all the row combinations (major, name) are unique. However, if there were more than one row with the same (major, name) value (e.g., ACC, ANDERSON), only one would be displayed.

YOUR TURN

Sections entitled *Your Turn* appear throughout the text after important topics are covered. These exercises are designed to reinforce your understanding of the preceding material. Answers to these exercises are found in Appendix E.

1. Develop a list of student IDs, names, sex codes, and majors.

2. Complete Example 3.2 again, this time displaying grade point average before major.

RETRIEVING A SUBSET OF ROWS: SIMPLE CONDITIONS

Often you don't want to retrieve all the rows in a table but want only the rows that satisify one or more conditions. In this case, you would include the WHERE clause in the SELECT statement to retrieve a portion, or subset, of the rows in a table.

A **search condition** expresses the logic by which the computer determines which rows of the table are retrieved and which are ignored. The search condition has many variations. A simple search condition is formed with a **conditional expression,** which specifies a comparison between two values. It has the following format:

| expression | comparison operator | expression | — Conditional expression. |

The expressions in the conditional expression are usually a column name or a constant. The comparison operator indicates a mathematical comparison such as less than, greater than, equal to, etc. Table 3.1 shows the comparison operators allowed in SQL.

TABLE 3.1 Comparison Operators

Type of Comparison	SQL Symbol
Equal to	=
Less than	<
Less than or equal to	<=
Greater than	>
Greater than or equal to	>=
Not equal to	<> or != or ¬=

For example, the conditional expression to find students with a GPA above 3.2 can be written

GPA > 3.2 ————————————————— **Numeric constant.**

The conditional expression to find all accounting majors is written

Character constants, sometimes called character strings, are enclosed in single quotes. ————

MAJOR = 'ACC'

The conditional expression can compare numeric values to one another or string values to one another as just shown.

Each row in the indicated table is evaluated, or tested, separately based on the condition in the WHERE clause. For each row, the evaluation of the conditional expression is either true or false. When a condition is true, a row is retrieved; when the condition is false, the row is not retrieved. For example, if an individual has a 3.5 GPA, then the conditional expression GPA > 3.2 is true and the row is included in the query result. However, if the individual had a GPA of 2.6, then the result of the conditional expression GPA > 3.2 is false and the row is not retrieved.

EXAMPLE 3.5   Develop a list of all accounting majors.

If you enter the SQL statement

```
SELECT   SNAME
FROM     STUDENT
WHERE    MAJOR = 'ACC' ──────────────────── Search condition.
                                            Character strings must
                                            be enclosed in quotes.
```

the result displayed on the screen will be

```
SNAME

RICHARDS
ANDERSON
```

In the WHERE clause, the condition "MAJOR must equal ACC" results in the retrieval of the name of each student majoring in accounting.

EXAMPLE 3.6   Develop a list of all students with a GPA above 3.25.

If you enter the statement

```
SELECT   SNAME, GPA
FROM     STUDENT
WHERE    GPA > 3.25 ─────────────── Numeric values are not
                                    enclosed in quotes.
```

the result displayed on the screen will be

```
SNAME          GPA

PELNICK        3.6
GAMBRELL       3.8
QUICK          3.5
ANDERSON       3.7
```

YOUR TURN	**3. a.** Retrieve the names and majors of all female students.
	b. Retrieve the names and majors of all students who are not accounting majors.
	4. Retrieve all the data on students who have a GPA of 2.5 or lower.

RETRIEVING A SUBSET OF ROWS: COMPOUND CONDITIONS

The conditions illustrated in the previous section are called simple conditions because each involves a single comparison. It is also possible to develop more complex conditions involving two or more conditional expressions. You combine conditions using the logical operators AND, OR, or NOT to connect conditional expressions. When two or more conditions are combined by logical operators, the conditional expression is called a **compound condition.** For example, you may want a list of males with a GPA above 3.0.

The form of the compound condition is

conditional	logical	conditional	logical	conditional	...
expression1	operator	expression2	operator	expression3	

As with simple conditional expressions, the evaluation of a compound condition is either true or false, with true resulting in retrieval of a row and false resulting in no retrieval.

Retrieval Using the AND Operator

When AND is used to connect two conditions, each conditional expression must be true for the compound condition to be true and the row retrieved. If any condition within a compound condition is false, the compound condition is false and the row is not selected.

For example, if you want to retrieve the records of male students with a GPA above 3.0, you can write the following compound condition:

———————————————————————— **Logical operator.**

SEX = 'M'   AND   GPA > 3.0

Table 3.2 illustrates the four possible cases that can occur with the logical operator AND for the compound condition just described.

TABLE 3.2   Logical Operator AND

| | Values for | | Condition1 | Condition2 | | |
	SEX	GPA	SEX = 'M'	GPA > 3.0	Yields	Row Result
Case 1	M	3.5	True	True	True	Retrieved
Case 2	M	2.5	True	False	False	Not retrieved
Case 3	F	3.2	False	True	False	Not retrieved
Case 4	F	2.8	False	False	False	Not retrieved

EXAMPLE 3.7   Develop a list of female students with a GPA above 3.25.

If you enter the statement

```
SELECT   SNAME, SEX, GPA
FROM     STUDENT
WHERE    SEX = 'F'  AND  GPA > 3.25
```

the result displayed on the screen will be

```
SNAME        SEX   GPA
PELNICK      F     3.6
GAMBRELL     F     3.8
QUICK        F     3.5
```

YOUR TURN   **5.** Retrieve the names and grade point averages of male finance majors.

6. List the names, sex, and grade point averages of all accounting majors with a GPA of 3.0 or higher.

Retrieval Using the OR Operator

When OR is used to connect two or more conditions, the compound condition is true if any condition is true, and the row is then retrieved. However, if all of the conditional expressions are false, then the row is not selected.

For example, suppose a recruiter is interested in either finance majors or any student with a GPA greater than or equal to 3.5. This compound condition can be written

                                                    ── Logical operator.

```
MAJOR = 'FIN'   OR   GPA >= 3.5
```

Table 3.3 illustrates the four possible cases that can occur with the logical operator OR for the example just given.

TABLE 3.2		Logical Operator OR				
	Values for		**Condition1**	**Condition2**		
	MAJOR	**GPA**	**MAJOR = 'FIN'**	**GPA > = 3.5**	**Yields**	**Row Result**
Case 1	FIN	3.9	True	True	True	Retrieved
Case 2	FIN	2.5	True	False	True	Retrieved
Case 3	ACC	3.7	False	True	True	Retrieved
Case 4	MKT	3.1	False	False	False	Not retrieved

EXAMPLE 3.8

A recruiter from a large brokerage firm wants to interview students majoring in finance or any student having a GPA above 3.2.

If you enter the statement

```
SELECT   SNAME, MAJOR, GPA
FROM     STUDENT
WHERE    MAJOR = 'FIN'  OR  GPA > 3.2
```

the result displayed on the screen will be

```
SNAME         MAJOR    GPA

PARKER        FIN      2.7
PELNICK       FIN      3.6
LEE           FIN      2.7
GAMBRELL      MKT      3.8
QUICK         MGT      3.5
ANDERSON      ACC      3.7
```

YOUR TURN

7. Retrieve the names, majors, and grade point averages of all students majoring in management (MGT) or accounting (ACC) or having a GPA above 3.0.

8. Retrieve the names and majors of all female students majoring in either finance (FIN) or marketing (MKT).

Retrieval Using Both AND and OR Operators

Compound conditions can include both AND and OR logical operators.

If you enter the query

```
SELECT   SNAME
FROM     STUDENT
WHERE    GPA > 3.5  AND  MAJOR = 'ACC'  OR  MAJOR = 'FIN'
```

the result displayed on the screen will be

```
SNAME

PARKER
PELNICK
LEE
ANDERSON
```

When you have a combination of AND and OR operators, the AND operators are evaluated first; then the OR operators are evaluated. Therefore, in the above query, rows from the STUDENT table are retrieved if they satisfy at least one of the following conditions:

1. The student is an accounting major with a GPA above 3.5.
2. The student is a finance major.

Retrieval Using Parentheses

Parentheses may be used within a compound condition to clarify or change the order in which the condition is evaluated. A condition within parentheses is evaluated before conditions outside the parentheses.

EXAMPLE 3.9   Retrieve the names, majors, and grade point averages of all students who have a GPA above 3.5 and who are majoring in either accounting or finance.

If you enter the query

```
SELECT   SNAME, MAJOR, GPA
FROM     STUDENT
WHERE    GPA > 3.5
  AND    ( MAJOR = 'ACC'  OR  MAJOR = 'FIN' )
```

the result displayed on the screen will be

```
SNAME         MAJOR    GPA

PELNICK       FIN      3.6
ANDERSON      ACC      3.7
```

(continued on next page)

This query retrieves rows from the STUDENT table that satisfy both of the following conditions:

1. The student has a GPA above 3.5.
2. The student majors in either accounting or finance.

Logical Operator NOT

The logical operator NOT allows the user to express conditions that are best expressed in a negative way. In essence, it reverses the logical value of a condition on which it operates. That is, it accepts all rows except those that satisfy the condition. You write the conditional expression with the keyword NOT preceding the condition:

```
WHERE   NOT   condition
```

The condition can be a simple condition or a condition containing ANDs and ORs. The compound condition using NOT is true if the condition following NOT is false; and the compound condition is false if the condition following NOT is true. For example, suppose you are looking for all students who are not accounting majors. You can write the conditional expression

NOT (MAJOR = 'ACC') ——————————————— **Parentheses are optional but are included
to improve readability
of the condition.**

If a student is a finance major, the computer evaluates the condition in the following manner:

Evaluation Process	Comments
Step 1: NOT (MAJOR = 'ACC')	Original condition.
Step 2: NOT ('FIN' = 'ACC')	Substitute FIN for MAJOR.
Step 3: NOT (false)	Since FIN does not equal ACC, the condition MAJOR = 'ACC' is false.
Step 4: true	NOT changes false to true, and the row is retrieved.

NOT is typically used with logical operators such as IN, BETWEEN, LIKE, etc., which will be covered in a later section.

In the query condition NOT (MAJOR = 'ACC'), you are more likely to write the condition as

```
                                    ┌──────────────────── Not equal to.
WHERE  MAJOR != 'ACC'
```

EXAMPLE 3.10   List all students except those majoring in marketing (MKT) and management (MGT).

If you enter the statement

```
SELECT   SNAME, MAJOR
FROM     STUDENT
WHERE    NOT ( MAJOR = 'MKT'  OR  MAJOR = 'MGT')
         └──────────────────────────────── NOT precedes the
                                            entire condition.
```

the result displayed on the screen will be

```
SNAME          MAJOR

PARKER         FIN
RICHARDS       ACC
PELNICK        FIN
LEE            FIN
ANDERSON       ACC
```

This statement retrieves the student name and major of each student whose major is not marketing or management.

YOUR TURN

9. Retrieve the names, majors, and grade point averages of all males who are majoring in accounting and have a GPA above 2.5.

10. List the names, sex, and grade point averages of marketing or management majors with a GPA above 3.5 or of finance majors who are female.

11. Use the NOT operator to write a query to list the names of all female students.

12. Rewrite Example 3.10 without using the NOT operator.

13. What is the output from the following query?

```
SELECT   SNAME
FROM     STUDENT
WHERE    GPA > 3.5  OR  MAJOR = 'ACC'  AND  MAJOR = 'FIN'
```

ADDITIONAL COMPARISON OPERATORS

SQL has four special comparison operators for use with search conditions. These operators are indicated by the keywords BETWEEN, IN, LIKE, and NULL.

Search Condition Using BETWEEN

The BETWEEN operator allows you to select rows of data in a given column if data in a given column contain values within a range. The general form of this operator is

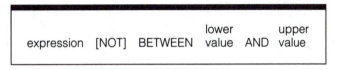

```
                              lower        upper
expression  [NOT]  BETWEEN    value   AND  value
```

The condition is true if the expression is greater than or equal to the lower value and less than or equal to the upper value. If the NOT operator is used, the row is retrieved if the expression is less than the lower value or greater than the upper value.

EXAMPLE 3.11 Find all students whose GPA is between 2.4 and 3.5.

If you enter the statement

```
SELECT  SNAME, GPA
FROM    STUDENT
WHERE   GPA  BETWEEN  2.4  AND  3.5
```

the result displayed on the screen will be

```
SNAME        GPA

POIRIER      3.2
PARKER       2.7
RICHARDS     2.4
MEGLIN       2.8
LEE          2.7
QUICK        3.5
```

The name of each student whose GPA is between 2.4 and 3.5 is retrieved. The limits include GPAs of 2.4 and 3.5. (Check the GPAs of RICHARDS and QUICK.

The AND logical operator can also be used to form a query that selects values from a range. A query similar to Example 3.11 would look like the following.

If you enter the statement

```
SELECT   SNAME, GPA
FROM     STUDENT
WHERE    GPA >= 2.4   AND   GPA <= 3.5
```

the result displayed on the screen will be

SNAME	GPA
POIRIER	3.2
PARKER	2.7
RICHARDS	2.4
MEGLIN	2.8
LEE	2.7
QUICK	3.5

Notice that the results are identical to the output in Example 3.11.

The BETWEEN operator can be modified with the logical operator NOT so that rows outside a range will be selected.

EXAMPLE 3.12   List the names of all students who do not have a GPA in the range of 2.4 to 3.5.

If you enter the statement

```
SELECT   SNAME, GPA
FROM     STUDENT
WHERE    GPA   NOT   BETWEEN   2.4   AND   3.5
```

the result displayed on the screen will be

SNAME	GPA
PELNICK	3.6
FAGIN	2.2
GAMBRELL	3.8
ANDERSON	3.7

This statement retrieves the names of all students with GPAs lower than 2.4 or higher than 3.5.

Search Condition Using IN

The IN operator is used when you want to select rows that match one of several listed values. If the row value matches any value in the list of values, the row is selected.

The format of this operator is

```
expression [NOT] IN (value1, value2, value3 ...)
```
— List of values.

— Enclose the entire list in parentheses.

— Separate items by commas.

EXAMPLE 3.13   List all students majoring in either accounting, management, or marketing.

If you enter the statement

```
SELECT   SNAME, MAJOR
FROM     STUDENT
WHERE    MAJOR IN ('ACC', 'MGT', 'MKT')
```

The row is retrieved if a student's major is in the set of majors.

the result displayed on the screen will be

SNAME	MAJOR
POIRIER	MGT
RICHARDS	ACC
FAGIN	MGT
MEGLIN	MGT
GAMBRELL	MKT
QUICK	MGT
ANDERSON	ACC

An equivalent query can be formed using the logical operator OR. It looks like the following:

```
SELECT   SNAME, MAJOR
FROM     STUDENT
WHERE    MAJOR = 'ACC'  OR  MAJOR = 'MGT'  OR  MAJOR = 'MKT'
```

The IN operator can be modified with the logical operator NOT.

EXAMPLE 3.14   List all students who are not majoring in either accounting or management.

If you enter the statement

```
SELECT   SNAME, MAJOR
FROM     STUDENT
WHERE    MAJOR  NOT IN ('ACC','MGT')
```

(continued on next page)

the result displayed on the screen will be

SNAME	MAJOR
PARKER	FIN
PELNICK	FIN
LEE	FIN
GAMBRELL	MKT

Search Condition Using LIKE

In SQL, a column value that contains character values can be matched to a pattern of characters for the purpose of retrieving one or more rows from a table. This is often referred to as **pattern matching.** Pattern matching is useful when a user cannot be specific about the data to be retrieved. For instance:

- You're not sure if an employee's last name is Robinson, Robertson, or Robbins. You search using the pattern "Rob".

- You want a list of all employees who live on Newman Avenue, Road, or Street. You search using the pattern "Newman".

- You want a list of all employees whose name ends in "man", such as Waterman, Spellman, or Herman. You search using the pattern "man".

The LIKE operator is used in the WHERE clause to enable you to retrieve records that have a partial match with a column value. The LIKE operator has the following format:

```
WHERE  column-name LIKE 'pattern'
```

COMMAND DISCUSSION

1. The column name following the WHERE clause must contain character values; otherwise, the LIKE operator cannot be used.

2. The LIKE operator compares the value in the specified column with the pattern. A row is retrieved if a match occurs.

3. The pattern can contain a string of characters including two special characters that are used to hide, or mask, characters in the string that you are not interested in comparing. These special characters are

   a. the percent (%) symbol, which means ignore zero or more characters in the string.

b. the underscore (_) symbol, which means ignore a single character in the string.

Table 3.4 illustrates the use of the LIKE operator with the special characters % and _.

TABLE 3.4	Use of Special Characters % and _ with the LIKE Operator	

Description of Situation	**SQL Clause**	**Pattern Being Searched For ***
Find all names that begin with "Rob".	WHERE SNAME LIKE 'Rob%'	Rob...
Find all employees living on Newman Avenue, Road, or Street.	WHERE ADDRS LIKE '%Newman%'	...Newman...
Find all names that end with "man".	WHERE SNAME LIKE '%man'	...man
Find all finance courses.	WHERE CRSNBR LIKE 'FIN_ _ _'	FIN _ _ _
Find all courses at the freshman level; i.e., numbers 100–199.	WHERE CRSNBR LIKE '_ _ _ 1%'	_ _ _ 1 ...

* Legend: ... means ignore all characters before and/or after pattern.
         _   means ignore a specific number of positions.

EXAMPLE 3.15   Retrieve the names of all students whose last name begins with "P".

If you enter the statement

```
SELECT  SNAME
FROM    STUDENT
WHERE   SNAME LIKE 'P%'
```
Ignores all characters after the first position in SNAME.

the result displayed on the screen will be

```
SNAME

POIRIER
PARKER
PELNICK
```

In this query, you are retrieving the names of all students whose name is "like" the pattern "P", followed by any other characters.

Search Condition Using NULL

Occasionally, when data are entered into a row, the value for one or more columns is unknown. For example, a new faculty member who doesn't have a phone extension assigned at the time the record is added to the FACULTY table has a null value stored in the phone extension column.

There are times when you wish to test for the presence or absence of null values in a specific column. The keywords IS NULL are used to find rows that contain null values in a specific column. The general form of this search condition is as follows:

```
column-name IS [NOT] NULL
```

NULL is used with the word IS instead of with the comparison operators = or !=. If a query to find null values is written in the form

```
WHERE column-name = NULL
```

no rows containing null values will be retrieved.

EXAMPLE 3.16   List the name of any student whose major is unknown (null).

If you enter the statement

```
SELECT   SNAME
FROM     STUDENT
WHERE    MAJOR IS NULL
```

the message displayed on the screen will be

```
No Records Selected
```

The search retrieved no records; that is, all the students currently have a major code assigned.

YOUR TURN

14. List the names and grade point averages of all accounting majors with a GPA between 2.9 and 3.6.

15. List the names and majors of all female students who major in either accounting, finance, or management.

16. List the names of all students whose name ends with "R".

17. List the names of all students whose name begins with "R" and ends with "S".

18. List the names of all students whose name has "R" as the third letter.

SORTING YOUR RESULTS

The output from the above queries may not be in the desired order. For example, you may want the list of students arranged alphabetically. Sorting is the process of rearranging data into some specific order. To sort the output into a desired sequence, a field or fields are specified that determine the order in which the results are arranged. These fields are called **sort keys.** For example, if the student data is sorted into student number sequence, then the student ID is the sort key. The name field is the sort key if the student table is sorted by name. Note that the sort key can be numeric (student ID) or character (student name).

Results can be sorted into ascending or descending sequence by sort key. Ascending means increasing order, and descending means decreasing order. For example, sorting the student table in ascending order by student ID means the student data will be arranged so that the student with the lowest ID is first and the student with the highest ID is last. If we sort the student table in descending order by grade point average, then the student record with the highest grade point average appears first, and the student record with the lowest grade point average is last.

Sorting character data in ascending or descending order is based on a coding, or collating, sequence assigned to numbers and letters by the computer. For example, when name is the sort key and you want the data arranged alphabetically, that indicates ascending order. If you want the data arranged in reverse alphabetical order, then specify descending order.

To sort your results using SQL, add the ORDER BY clause to the SELECT statement. The form of this clause is

```
ORDER BY  column-name  [DESC]
```

where DESC indicates the rows are to be arranged in descending order. If DESC is omitted, your output is sorted in ascending order.

This clause fits into the SELECT expression following the WHERE clause, as shown below:

```
SELECT      column-name1 [, column-name2] ...
FROM        table-name
[WHERE      search-condition]
[ORDER BY   column-name  [DESC] ]
```

EXAMPLE 3.17   Retrieve a list of students in alphabetical order.

If you enter the statement

```
SELECT      SNAME, MAJOR, GPA
FROM        STUDENT
ORDER BY    SNAME ──────────────────────── Output will be
                                            arranged alphabeti-
                                            cally by student name.
```

the result displayed on the screen will be

SNAME	MAJOR	GPA
ANDERSON	ACC	3.7
FAGIN	MGT	2.2
GAMBRELL	MKT	3.8
LEE	FIN	2.7
MEGLIN	MGT	2.8
PARKER	FIN	2.7
PELNICK	FIN	3.6
POIRIER	MGT	3.2
QUICK	MGT	3.5
RICHARDS	ACC	2.4

EXAMPLE 3.18   Retrieve a list of all students with a GPA above 3.0, placing the student with the highest grade point average first.

If you enter the statement

```
            SELECT      SNAME, MAJOR, GPA
            FROM        STUDENT
            WHERE       GPA > 3.0
            ORDER BY    GPA DESC
```

Output will be arranged by GPA in descending order.

(continued on next page)

the result displayed on the screen will be

SNAME	MAJOR	GPA
GAMBRELL	MKT	3.8
ANDERSON	ACC	3.7
PELNICK	FIN	3.6
QUICK	MGT	3.5
POIRIER	MGT	3.2

Sometimes you may want to arrange your data by more than one attribute. For example, you may wish to sort the student data by major and then alphabetically by name within each major. Now you have two sort keys. Sorting with multiple keys is accomplished by specifying in the ORDER BY clause each column you want to sort. The format is

```
ORDER BY  column-name1 [DESC] [, column-name2 [DESC] ] ...
```

Multiple sort keys are listed in the order in which sorting is to be done. Thus, if you want data arranged by major and then alphabetically by name within each major, the ORDER BY clause would list the MAJOR column first, followed by the SNAME column. In all cases, the column or columns being ordered must appear in the SELECT clause.

EXAMPLE 3.19   Retrieve a list of students arranged by major and, within major, arranged by the highest grade point average first.

If you enter the statement

```
SELECT     SNAME, MAJOR, GPA
FROM       STUDENT
ORDER BY   MAJOR, GPA DESC
```

Output will appear in ascending order automatically if DESC is omitted.

the result displayed on the screen will be

SNAME	MAJOR	GPA
ANDERSON	ACC	3.7
RICHARDS	ACC	2.4

(continued on next page)

PELNICK	FIN	3.6
PARKER	FIN	2.7
LEE	FIN	2.7
QUICK	MGT	3.5
POIRIER	MGT	3.2
MEGLIN	MGT	2.8
FAGIN	MGT	2.2
GAMBRELL	MKT	3.8

Notice that all students in the same major are listed together, with the majors listed in ascending order. Within each major, the student with the highest grade point average is listed first.

On many SQL implementations, it is possible to have as many as 16 sort keys. The order in which the sort keys are listed is the order in which the data will be arranged.

Sort keys can also be specified by using relative position numbers instead of column names. In this case, a number following the keywords ORDER BY indicates the item or items on which to sort. The relative position number refers to the position of an item in the SELECT clause. The first item is assigned position number 1, the second item is assigned position number 2, and so on. The ability to use numbers as sort keys is most helpful when you sort on a calculated field. (This will be covered in Chapter 4.)

EXAMPLE 3.20   List the names, grade point averages, and majors of all students on the Dean's list (GPA of 3.25 or above). Arrange the output so that the student with the highest grade point average appears first.

If you enter the statement

```
                                                    ┌──────── Relative position 1.
                        ┌──────────────── Relative position 2.
SELECT     SNAME, GPA, MAJOR
FROM       STUDENT          └──────────── Relative position 3.
WHERE      GPA > 3.25
ORDER BY   2 DESC
           └────────────── Second item in the
                           SELECT clause.
```

the result displayed on the screen will be

SNAME	GPA	MAJOR
GAMBRELL	3.8	MKT
ANDERSON	3.7	ACC

(continued on next page)

```
PELNICK        3.6        FIN
QUICK          3.5        MGT
```

Note that the ORDER BY clause contains a number instead of a column name. The number refers to the second position in the SELECT clause.

YOUR TURN

19. List the student IDs and names of all students. Arrange the list by student ID (lowest ID first).

20. List the names, majors, and grade point averages of all students with a GPA above 3.0. Arrange the list by major and, within major, arrange the list by GPA (highest GPA first).

21. List the names and sex of all students. Arrange the list by sex and, within sex, sort the names alphabetically.

This chapter introduced several ways to retrieve rows and columns from a table. In the next chapter, you will learn how to perform calculations on data stored in a table.

Video Rental, Inc. Case
CHAPTER ASSIGNMENT

1. Retrieve a list of the names of the members. Arrange the list alphabetically.

2. **a.** Retrieve the titles and categories of all the movies. Arrange the list by category and, within category, by title.

   b. Retrieve the titles, ratings, and categories of all movies. Arrange the list by rating; within rating, by category; and within category, by title.

3. List the movie category codes. (Don't repeat any codes.)

4. Retrieve the names and addresses of all annual members.

5. Retrieve the titles and ratings of all action movies (AC) with a "PG13" rating.

6. Retrieve the titles and ratings of all movies rated either "PG" or "G." Arrange the list by title.

7. List the titles, ratings, and categories of all but the "R"-rated movies. Arrange the list by rating and, within rating, by title.

8. Retrieve the titles, ratings, and categories of all comedy, horror, or action movies available to rent. Arrange the results by rating and then by title.

9. Retrieve the member ID, invoice number, and date rented for invoices 10560 to 10565 inclusive.

10. Prepare a list of the titles and dates purchased for any movie purchased in March, 1987.

11. List the titles of all action movies (AC) rated "PG13" that are available for rental.

12. **a.** List the movies (title and movie ID) rated either "G" or "PG," except those in the children's category.

    b. From the list in 12a, retrieve only those movies in the store.

13. List the title of any movie with the word "Fly" in the title.

Chapter 4

Queries Involving Calculated Values

To illustrate the material in this chapter, the FACULTY table will be used. The university stores data about faculty to aid in budgeting, class scheduling, and reporting. The table contains the following data: faculty ID, name, phone extension, department code, salary, and rank. A list of the faculty data follows:

FID	FNAME	EXT	DEPT	RANK	SALARY
036	BARGES	325	MGT	ASSO	35000
117	JARDIN	212	FIN	FULL	33000
098	KENNEDY	176	ACC	ASSO	30000
075	SAMPLE	171	MKT	ASST	25000
138	WARD	125	MGT	INST	20000
219	PETERS	220	FIN	FULL	45000
151	DARDEN	250	ACC	ASSO	37000
113	PIERCE	205	MGT	INST	22000

ARITHMETIC CALCULATIONS

This section covers the computational features of SQL. While limited, they do allow the user to perform computations on the data and/or retrieve rows based on conditions involving computations. For example, you can adjust salaries for a 5 percent across-the-board increase, or you can compute weekly salaries (i.e., salary divided by 52).

Arithmetic calculations are performed on fields, or columns, in the database. An **arithmetic expression** is used to describe the desired computation. The expression consists of column names and numeric constants connected by parentheses and arithmetic operators. Table 4.1 shows the arithmetic operators used in SQL.

	Arithmetic Operation	SQL Operator	Example
TABLE 4.1	Arithmetic Operators		
	Addition	+	SALARY + 2000
	Subtraction	–	SALARY – 1000
	Multiplication	*	SALARY * 1.05
	Division	/	SALARY / 26

Typically, the arithmetic expression is used in the SELECT clause to perform calculations on data stored in the table.

EXAMPLE 4.1   Next year every faculty member will receive a 5 percent salary increase. List the names of each faculty member, his or her current salary, and next year's salary.

The statement

```
                                                    ┌──────────── Arithmetic
                                                    │            expression.
SELECT   FNAME, SALARY, SALARY * 1.05
FROM     FACULTY
```

results in

FNAME	SALARY	SALARY * 1.05
BARGES	35000	36750
JARDIN	33000	34650
KENNEDY	30000	31500
SAMPLE	25000	26250
WARD	20000	21000
PETERS	45000	47250
DARDEN	37000	38850
PIERCE	22000	23100

The expression "SALARY * 1.05" results in each value in the salary column being multiplied by 1.05. The results are then displayed in a new column that is labeled SALARY * 1.05.

If more than one arithmetic operator is used in an arithmetic expression, parentheses can be used to control the order in which the arithmetic calculations are performed. The operations enclosed in parentheses are computed before operations that are not enclosed in parentheses. For example, the expression

    12 * (SALARY + BONUS)

means bonus is added to salary, and then this result is multiplied by 12.

If parentheses are omitted or if several operations are included within the parentheses, the order in which calculations are performed is as follows:

- First, all multiplication and division operations are performed.
- Then, all addition and subtraction operations are performed.

For example, in the expression

    SALARY + SALARY * .05

the value in the SALARY column is multiplied by .05, and then the salary value is added to this intermediate result.

When two or more computations in an expression are at the same level (e.g., multiplication and division), the operations are executed from left to right. For example, in the expression

    SALARY / 12 * 1.05

the salary value is first divided by 12, and then this result is multiplied by 1.05.

Arithmetic calculation can also be used in a WHERE clause to select rows based on a calculated condition. In addition, arithmetic expressions can be used in the HAVING and ORDER BY clauses, which will be discussed in later sections of this chapter.

EXAMPLE 4.2   List the names of all faculty members earning a monthly salary above $3,000.

The query

```
SELECT  FNAME
FROM    FACULTY
WHERE   (SALARY/12) > 3000
```

results in

    FNAME

    PETERS
    DARDEN

The rows in the FACULTY table are retrieved if the condition "salary divided by 12" is greater than $3,000.

YOUR TURN

1. Modify Example 4.1 so that the difference between the proposed salary increase and the current salary is also displayed.

2. List all faculty names and their biweekly salaries, which cover 26 pay periods. Sort the results by descending biweekly amounts.

3. List the names of faculty members whose biweekly salary is less than $1,000.

SUMMARIZING VALUES: GROUP BY CLAUSE AND AGGREGATE FUNCTIONS

So far, the examples presented have shown how to retrieve and manipulate values from individual rows in a table. In this section, we will illustrate how summary information can be obtained from groups of rows in a table.

Often we find it useful to group data by some characteristic of the group, such as major, department, or rank, so that summary statistics (totals, averages, etc.) about the group can be calculated. For example, to calculate average departmental salaries, the user could group the salaries of all faculty members by department. In SQL, the GROUP BY clause is used to divide the rows of a table into groups that have matching values in one or more columns. The form of this clause is

```
GROUP BY column-name1  [, column-name2] ...
```

and it fits into the SELECT expression in the following manner:

```
SELECT      column-name1 [, column-name2] ...
FROM        table-name
[WHERE      search-condition]
[GROUP BY   column-name1 [, column-name2] ...]
[ORDER BY   column-name1 [DESC] [, column-name2 [DESC] ] ...
```

The column(s) listed in the GROUP BY clause are used to form groups. The grouping is based on rows with the same value in the specified column or columns being placed in the same group. It is important to note that grouping is conceptual—the table is not physically rearranged.

The GROUP BY clause is normally used along with five built-in, or "aggregate," functions. These functions perform special operations on an entire table or on a set, or group, of rows rather than on each row and then return one row of values for each group. Table 4.2 lists the aggregate functions available with SQL.

TABLE 4.2	SQL Aggregate Function Names	
Function Name	**Meaning**	**Example**
SUM(column name)	Total of the values in a numeric column	SUM(SALARY)
AVG(column name)	Average of the values in a column	AVG(SALARY)
MAX(column name)	Largest value in a column	MAX(SALARY)
MIN(column name)	Smallest value in a column	MIN(SALARY)
COUNT(*)	Count of the number of rows selected	COUNT(*)

Aggregate functions are used in place of column names in the SELECT statement. The form of the function is

Function name (argument)

In all situations except for the function COUNT, the argument represents the column name to which the function applies. For example, if the sum of all salaries is needed, then the function SUM is used and the argument is the column SALARY. When COUNT is used, no column name is needed because the function does not apply to a specific column. An asterisk (*) is placed within the parentheses instead of a column name.

EXAMPLE 4.3   What is the average salary paid in each department?

The statement

                                                                 Aggregate function
                                                                 name.

    SELECT   DEPT, AVG(SALARY)
    FROM   FACULTY   Column on which
    GROUP BY   DEPT   average is computed.

Group rows by department.

(continued on next page)

results in

DEPT	AVG(SALARY)
ACC	33500
FIN	39000
MGT	25666.6667
MKT	25000

Note that individual faculty rows are not displayed.

In this query, all rows in the FACULTY table that have the same department codes are grouped together. The aggregate function AVG is calculated for the salary column in each group. The department code and the average departmental salary are displayed for each department.

A SELECT clause that contains an aggregate function cannot contain any column name that does not apply to a group; for example:

The statement

```
SELECT     FNAME, AVG(SALARY)
FROM       FACULTY
GROUP BY   DEPT
```

FNAME references an individual row; also FNAME is not included in GROUP BY clause.

results in the message

Error at Line 1: Not a GROUP BY Expression

It is not permissible to include column names in a SELECT clause that are not referenced in the GROUP BY clause. The only column names that can be displayed, along with aggregate functions, must be listed in the GROUP BY clause. Since FNAME is not included in the GROUP BY clause, an error message results.

EXAMPLE 4.4   The chair of the Accounting Department plans to participate in a national salary survey for faculty in Accounting Departments. Determine the average salary paid to the Accounting faculty.

The statement

```
SELECT   COUNT(*), AVG(SALARY)
FROM     FACULTY
WHERE    DEPT = 'ACC'
```

(continued on next page)

results in

COUNT(*)	AVG(SALARY)
2	33500

In this example, the aggregate function AVG is used in a SELECT statement that has a WHERE clause. SQL selects the rows that represent Accounting faculty and then applies the aggregate function to these rows.

You can divide the rows of a table into groups based on values in more than one column. For example, you might want to compute total salary by department and then, within a department, want subtotals by faculty rank.

EXAMPLE 4.5   What is the total salary paid by rank in each department?

The statement

```
SELECT     DEPT, RANK, SUM(SALARY)
FROM       FACULTY
GROUP BY   DEPT, RANK
```
Grouping by department and, within department, by rank.

results in

DEPT	RANK	SUM(SALARY)
ACC	ASSO	67000
FIN	FULL	78000
MGT	ASSO	35000
MGT	INST	42000
MKT	ASST	25000

Separate average for each rank within MGT.

In this query, the rows are grouped by department and, within each department, faculty with the same rank are grouped so that totals can be computed. Notice that the columns DEPT and RANK can appear in the SELECT statement since both columns appear in the GROUP BY clause.

If the GROUP BY clause is omitted when an aggregate function is used, then the entire table is considered as one group, and the group function displays a single value for the entire table.

EXAMPLE 4.6   What is the total salary paid to the faculty?

The statement

```
SELECT   SUM(SALARY)
FROM     FACULTY
```

results in

```
SUM(SALARY)

247000
```

YOUR TURN

4. What is the total salary paid in each department? Display the department and total salary.

5. What is the highest salary in the university?

6. What is the average salary paid at each faculty rank? Also include the number of faculty members in each rank and the rank code.

7. Arrange the answer to the previous exercise in descending order by average salary.

8. What is the total salary paid to faculty members in the Accounting Department?

9. How many associate professors (ASSO) are there in each department?

10. Using the STUDENT table, what is the average GPA by major? Arrange the results from highest average GPA to lowest average GPA.

GROUPS WITH CONDITIONS: HAVING CLAUSE

Sometimes you may want to specify a condition that applies to groups rather than to individual rows. For example, you might want a list of departments where the average departmental salary is above $25,000. To express such a query, the HAVING clause is used. This clause specifies which groups should be selected and is used in combination with the GROUP BY clause. The form of this clause is as follows:

```
[ GROUP BY   column-name1 [, column-name2] ...
[ HAVING     search-condition ]
```

Conditions in the HAVING clause are applied after groups are formed. The search condition of the HAVING clause examines the grouped rows and produces a row for each group where the search condition in the HAVING clause is true. The clause is similar to the WHERE clause, except the HAVING clause applies to groups.

EXAMPLE 4.7

Which departments have an average salary above $25,000? Order the results by average salary, with highest average salary appearing first.

The statement

```
SELECT      DEPT, AVG(SALARY)
FROM        FACULTY
GROUP BY    DEPT
HAVING      AVG(SALARY) > 25000 ─────────── When HAVING is used,
ORDER BY    2  DESC                          it always follows a
                                             GROUP BY clause.
```

results in   Computed value
                                             (average salary) is
                                             basis of sort.

DEPT	AVG(SALARY)
FIN	39000
ACC	33500
MGT	25666.6667

In this query, the average salary for all departments is computed, but only the names of those departments having an average salary above $25,000 are displayed. Notice that the Marketing (MKT) Department's average of $25,000 is not displayed.

The GROUP BY clause does not sort the results, thus the need for the ORDER BY clause. Finally, note that the ORDER BY clause must be placed after the GROUP BY and HAVING clauses.

YOUR TURN

Use the STUDENT table to answer these questions.

11. List the average GPA for each major. Which majors have a GPA above 3.0?

12. List the majors in which more than two students are enrolled.

This chapter has covered the computational capabilities of SQL. In the next chapter, you will learn how to develop more complex queries by using the join operation and the nesting of queries.

Video Rental, Inc. Case
CHAPTER ASSIGNMENT

1. **a.** What are the total costs of all movies purchased?

   b. Summarize these costs by movie category.

2. **a.** Count the number of times each movie has been rented. Display the movie ID and the count, with the movie rented most often appearing first.

   b. Which movies have been rented more than once? Display the movie ID.

3. What is the average purchase price Video Rentals pays for its movies?

4. **a.** How many life-time members are in the club?

   b. How much money was collected from life-time members?

Chapter 5

Advanced Queries

This chapter is divided into three sections. The first one focuses on using the join operation to retrieve data from multiple tables. The second section covers nesting of queries, also known as subqueries. The final section introduces several advanced query techniques, including self-joins, correlated subqueries, subqueries using the EXIST operator, and combining query results using the UNION operator.

RETRIEVING DATA FROM MULTIPLE TABLES

All the queries looked at so far have been answered by accessing data from one table. Sometimes, however, answers to a query may require data from two or more tables. For example, to display a student's class schedule, including student name and course number, requires data from the CRSENRL table (course number) and data from the STUDENT table (student name). Obtaining the data you need requires the ability to combine two or more tables. This process is commonly referred to as "joining the tables."

Two or more tables can be combined to form a single table by using the **join operation.** The join operation is based on the premise that there is a logical association between two tables based on a common attribute that links the tables. Therefore, there must be a common column in each table for a join operation to be executed. For example, both the FACULTY table and the COURSE table have the faculty identification number in common. Thus, they can be joined.

Joining two tables in SQL is accomplished by using a SELECT statement. The general form of the SELECT statement when a join operation is involved is

Join condition. ⎯⎯⎯⎯⎯⎯⎯

```
SELECT   column-name1 [, column-name2] ...
FROM     table-name1, table-name2
WHERE    table-name1.column-name = table-name2.column-name
```

COMMAND DISCUSSION

1. A join operation pulls data from two or more tables listed in the FROM clause. These tables represent the source of the data to be joined.

2. The WHERE clause specifies the relationship between the tables to be joined. This relationship represents the **join condition.** Typically, the join condition expresses a relationship between rows from each table that match on a common attribute.

3. When the tables to be joined have the same column name, the column name is prefixed with a table name in order for SQL to know from which table the column comes. SQL uses the notation

   table-name.column-name

   The table name in front of the column name is referred to as a **qualifier.**

4. The common attributes in the join condition need not have the same column name, but they should represent the same kind of information. For example, the attribute representing the faculty identification number could be named FID in table 1, while the identification number is named FAC_NO in table 2. In this case, you could still join the tables on the common faculty identification number attribute by specifying

   WHERE table-name1.FID = table-name2.FAC_NO

5. If a row from one of the tables never satisfies the join condition, that row will not appear in the joined table.

6. The tables are joined together, and then SQL extracts the data, or columns, listed in the SELECT clause.

7. Although tables can be combined if you omit the WHERE clause, this would result in a table of all possible combinations of rows from the tables in the FROM clause. This output is usually not intended, nor meaningful, and can waste much computer processing time. Therefore, be careful in forming queries that involve multiple tables.

EXAMPLE 5.1   The registrar wants to distribute a list of courses, along with the name of the faculty member teaching the course. To fulfill this request, data from both the COURSE table (course number and course name) and the FACULTY table (faculty name) are needed.

(continued on next page)

The statement

```
SELECT   CRSNBR, CNAME, FNAME
FROM     FACULTY, COURSE ──────────────── Tables to be joined.
WHERE    FACULTY.FID = COURSE.FID ──────── Condition for the join.
```

Qualifier indicates
from which table. ─────────────────────

results in the following joined table:

CRSNBR	CNAME	FNAME
MGT681	INTERNATIONAL MGT	BARGES
FIN601	MANAGERIAL FINANCE	JARDIN
ACC661	TAXATION	KENNEDY
ACC610	BASIC ACCOUNTING	KENNEDY
MKT610	MKTING FOR MANAGERS	SAMPLE
MKT670	PRODUCT MARKETING	SAMPLE
MGT630	INTRO TO MANAGEMENT	WARD
FIN602	INVESTMENT SKILLS	PETERS

These columns came
from the COURSE ──────────────────────
table.

This column came from
the FACULTY table.

In this query, we are joining data from the FACULTY and COURSE tables. The common attribute in these two tables is the faculty ID (FID). The conditional expression

FACULTY.FID = COURSE.FID

is used to describe how the rows in the two tables are to be matched. Each row of the joined table is the result of combining a row from the FACULTY table and a row from the COURSE table for each comparison with matching IDs.

To further illustrate how the join works, look at the shaded rows (FID = 098) in the FACULTY table (Figure 5.1a) and in the COURSE table (Figure 5.1b). These are matching rows since the faculty ID (098) is the same. The matching rows can be conceptualized as combining a row from the FACULTY table with a matching row from the COURSE table (Figure 5.1c). This operation is carried out for all matching rows; i.e., each row in the FACULTY table is combined, or matched, with a row having the same FID in the COURSE table (Figure 5.1d).

Observe that the joined table (Figure 5.1d) does not include any data on two faculty members from the FACULTY table (DARDEN and PIERCE). The joined table includes only rows where a match has occurred between rows in both tables. If a row in either table does not match any row in the other table, the row is not included in the joined table.

In addition, notice that the FID column is not included in the final joined table (Figure 5.1e). Only three columns are included in the joined table since just three columns are listed in the SELECT clause, and FID is not one of them.

FIGURE 5.1a   FACULTY Table

FID	FNAME	EXT	DEPT	RANK	SALARY
036	BARGES	325	MGT	ASSO	35000
117	JARDIN	212	FIN	FULL	33000
098	KENNEDY	176	ACC	ASSO	30000
075	SAMPLE	171	MKT	ASST	25000
138	WARD	125	MGT	INST	20000
219	PETERS	220	FIN	FULL	45000
151	DARDEN	250	ACC	ASSO	37000
113	PIERCE	205	MGT	INST	22000

FIGURE 5.1b   COURSE Table

CRSNBR	CNAME	CREDIT	MAXENRL	FID
MGT630	INTRO TO MANAGEMENT	4	30	138
FIN601	MANAGERIAL FINANCE	4	25	117
MKT610	MKTING FOR MANAGERS	3	35	075
ACC661	TAXATION	3	30	098
FIN602	INVESTMENT SKILLS	3	25	219
ACC610	BASIC ACCOUNTING	4	25	098
MGT681	INTERNATIONAL MGT	3	20	036
MKT670	PRODUCT MARKETING	3	20	075

FIGURE 5.1c   Sample of Matching Rows from FACULTY and COURSE Tables

FID	FNAME	EXT	DEPT	RANK	SALARY	CRSNBR	CNAME	CREDIT	MAXENRL
098	KENNEDY	176	ACC	ASSO	30000	ACC661	TAXATION	3	30
098	KENNEDY	176	ACC	ASSO	30000	ACC610	BASIC ACCOUNTING	4	25

FIGURE 5.1d   Matching All Rows from FACULTY and COURSE Tables

FID	FNAME	EXT	DEPT	RANK	SALARY	CRSNBR	CNAME	CREDIT	MAXENRL
036	BARGES	325	MGT	ASSO	35000	MGT681	INTERNATIONAL MGT	3	20
117	JARDIN	212	FIN	FULL	33000	FIN601	MANAGERIAL FINANCE	4	25
098	KENNEDY	176	ACC	ASSO	30000	ACC661	TAXATION	3	30
098	KENNEDY	176	ACC	ASSO	30000	ACC610	BASIC ACCOUNTING	4	25
075	SAMPLE	171	MKT	ASST	25000	MKT670	PRODUCT MARKETING	3	20
075	SAMPLE	171	MKT	ASST	25000	MKT610	MKTING FOR MANAGERS	3	35
138	WARD	125	MGT	INST	20000	MGT630	INTRO TO MANAGEMENT	4	30
219	PETERS	220	FIN	FULL	45000	FIN602	INVESTMENT SKILLS	3	25

FIGURE 5.1e	Joined Table

CRSNBR	CNAME	FNAME
MGT681	INTERNATIONAL MGT	BARGES
FIN601	MANAGERIAL FINANCE	JARDIN
ACC661	TAXATION	KENNEDY
ACC610	BASIC ACCOUNTING	KENNEDY
MKT610	MKTING FOR MANAGERS	SAMPLE
MKT670	PRODUCT MARKETING	SAMPLE
MGT630	INTRO TO MANAGEMENT	WARD
FIN602	INVESTMENT SKILLS	PETERS

The next example illustrates that conditions other than the join condition can be used in the WHERE clause. It also shows that even though the results come from a single table, the solution may require that data from two or more tables be joined in the WHERE clause.

EXAMPLE 5.2

In which courses is FAGIN enrolled? (Assume that you cannot remember FAGIN's student ID.)

The statement

```
SELECT   CRSNBR
FROM     STUDENT, CRSENRL ───────────────── Tables to be joined.
WHERE    SNAME = 'FAGIN'
   AND   STUDENT.SID = CRSENRL.SID ────────── Condition for the join
                                              operation.
```

results in

```
CRSNBR

MKT610
MKT670
ACC610
```

Since you don't know FAGIN's ID number, you use the student's name found in the STUDENT table in order to find the row that stores FAGIN's ID. Conceptually, visualize the join operation to occur as follows:

1. The conditional expression SNAME = 'FAGIN' references one row from the STUDENT table; i.e., FAGIN's row.

2. Now that FAGIN's ID is known, this row in the STUDENT table is joined with the rows in the CRSENRL table that have SID = 862. The joined table represents the numbers of the courses in which FAGIN is enrolled.

As the next example illustrates, more than two tables can be joined together.

EXAMPLE 5.3   Provide a class roster of students enrolled in FIN601. The report should include the course number, course name, and student name.

The statement

```
SELECT   COURSE.CRSNBR, CNAME, SNAME
FROM     COURSE, CRSENRL, STUDENT
WHERE    COURSE.CRSNBR = 'FIN601'
AND      COURSE.CRSNBR = CRSENRL.CRSNBR
AND      CRSENRL.SID = STUDENT.SID
```

The order of the joins in the WHERE clause is not important.

— **Tables joined.**

— **Condition for joining COURSE and CRSENRL.**

— **Condition for joining CRSENRL and STUDENT.**

results in

CRSNBR	CNAME	SNAME
FIN601	MANAGERIAL FINANCE	PARKER
FIN601	MANAGERIAL FINANCE	MEGLIN

In this example, data from three tables (COURSE, CRSENRL, and STUDENT) are joined together. Conceptually, the COURSE table references the row that contains FIN601; this gives us the course name, MANAGERIAL FINANCE. The course number, FIN601, is joined with all rows in the CRSENRL table that have CRSNBR equal to FIN601. This yields the intermediate table-1 (shown below) containing all the columns from both the COURSE and CRSENRL tables.

Intermediate Table–1

CRSNBR	CNAME	CREDIT	MAXENRL	FID	SID	GRADE
FIN601	MANAGERIAL FINANCE	4	25	117	763	B
FIN601	MANAGERIAL FINANCE	4	25	117	748	A

This intermediate table is joined with the STUDENT table, based on the join condition

```
CRSENRL.SID = STUDENT.SID
```

to form

(continued on next page)

Intermediate Table–2

CRSNBR	CNAME	CREDIT	MAXENRL	FID	SID	GRADE	SNAME	SEX	MAJOR	GPA
FIN601	MANAGERIAL FINANCE	4	25	117	763	B	PARKER	F	FIN	2.7
FIN601	MANAGERIAL FINANCE	4	25	117	748	A	MEGLIN	M	MGT	2.8

Finally, the SELECT clause indicates the columns that you want displayed. The course number, course name, and student name are displayed as follows:

CRSNBR	CNAME	SNAME
FIN601	MANAGERIAL FINANCE	PARKER
FIN601	MANAGERIAL FINANCE	MEGLIN

As a final point, the order in which you place the conditions in the WHERE clause does not affect the way SQL accesses the data. SQL contains an "optimizer," that is, sophisticated software, which chooses the best access path to the data based on factors such as index availability, size of tables involved, number of unique values in an indexed column, and other statistical information. Thus, the results would not be affected by writing the same query in the following order:

```
SELECT  COURSE.CRSNBR, CNAME, SNAME
FROM    COURSE, CRSENRL, STUDENT
WHERE   CRSENRL.SID = STUDENT.SID
  AND   COURSE.CRSNBR = CRSENRL.CRSNBR
  AND   COURSE.CRSNBR = 'FIN601'
```

YOUR TURN

1. What is the result of the following query?

```
SELECT  CRSNBR, CNAME
FROM    CRSENRL, COURSE
WHERE   CRSENRL.CRSNBR = COURSE.CRSNBR
  AND   SID = '862'
```

2. Prepare a grade report for each student. Include the student ID, student name, course number, and grade.

3. Modify the above grade report to include the course name.

4. Modify Example 5.3 so that the course roster for FIN601 includes the name of the faculty member teaching the course.

NESTING QUERIES

At times you may wish to retrieve rows in one table based on conditions in a related table. For example, suppose the Dean of Students needs to call in all students who received a grade of "F" to counsel them. To answer this query, you have to retrieve the names of all students, found in the STUDENT table, based on data found in the CRSENRL table (grades of students). In other situations, you may want to formulate a query from one table that requires you to make two passes through the table in order to obtain the desired results. For example, you may want to retrieve a list of faculty members earning a salary higher than Peters, but you don't know Peters' salary. To answer this query, you first find Peters' salary; then you compare the salary of each faculty member to Peters' salary.

One approach is to develop a **subquery**, which involves embedding a query (SELECT-FROM-WHERE block) within the WHERE clause of another query. This is sometimes referred to as a "nested query."

The format of a nested query is

Outer query.

```
SELECT   column-name1 [,column-name2] ...
FROM     table-name
WHERE    column-name IN
```

Subquery.

```
( SELECT   column-name
  FROM     table-name
  WHERE    search-condition )
```

The IN operator is normally used if the inner query returns many rows and one column.

Here are some points concerning the use of nested queries:

1. The above SQL statement contains two SELECT-FROM-WHERE blocks. The portion in parentheses is called the subquery. The subquery is evaluated first; then the outer query is evaluated based on the result of the subquery. In effect, the nested query can be looked at as being equivalent to

```
SELECT   column-name1 [,column-name2] ...
FROM     table-name
WHERE    column-name  IN  ( set of values from the subquery )
```

    where the set of values is determined from the inner SELECT-FROM-WHERE block.

2. The IN operator is used to link the outer query to the subquery when the subquery returns a set of values (one or more). Other comparison operators, such as <, >, =, etc., can be used to link an outer query to a subquery when the subquery returns a single value.

3. The subquery must have only a single column or expression in the SELECT clause.

4. You are not limited to one subquery. On some implementations of SQL, subqueries can be nested up to 16 levels. Any of the operators (IN, =, <, >, etc.) can be used to link the subquery to the next higher level.

5. You can use a subquery only if the values in the outer, or main, query come from a single table. If the desired output comes from more than one table, a join operation is required.

EXAMPLE 5.4   List the names of all students enrolled in FIN601.

The statement

```
SELECT  SNAME
FROM    STUDENT
WHERE   SID IN

    ( SELECT  SID
      FROM    CRSENRL                          ——————— Subquery.
      WHERE   CRSNBR = 'FIN601' ) ——————— Parentheses are placed
                                              around the subquery.
```

results in

```
SNAME

PARKER
MEGLIN
```

To understand how this expression retrieves its results, work from the bottom up in evaluating the SELECT statement. In other words, the subquery is evaluated first. This results in a set of values that can be used as the basis for the outer query. The innermost SELECT block retrieves the following set of student IDs: 763, 748.

In the outermost SELECT block, the IN operator tests whether any student ID in the STUDENT table is contained in the set of student ID values retrieved from the inner SELECT block; i.e., 748 or 763.

In effect, the outer SELECT block is equivalent to

```
SELECT  SNAME
FROM    STUDENT                              Values from the
WHERE   SID IN (748,763) ——————— subquery.
```

Thus, the student names PARKER and MEGLIN are retrieved.

Subqueries can be nested several levels deep within a query, as the next example illustrates.

EXAMPLE 5.5   List the name of any student enrolled in INTRO TO MANAGEMENT who received an "F" in the course.

The statement

```
SELECT   SNAME
FROM     STUDENT
WHERE    SID IN ─────────────────────────

    ( SELECT   SID
      FROM     CRSENRL
      WHERE    GRADE = 'F'
      AND      CRSNBR = ──────────────────────

          ( SELECT   CRSNBR
            FROM     COURSE
            WHERE    CNAME = 'INTRO TO MANAGEMENT') )
```

IN is used here since it's possible to retrieve several SID values.

= is used here since only one course number is retrieved; although, IN can also be used.

results in

SNAME

PELNICK

Again, remember that a nested query is evaluated from the bottom up; i.e., from the innermost query to the outermost query. First, the course number for INTRO TO MANAGEMENT is retrieved (MGT630) from the COURSE table. Once the CRSNBR is known, the CRSENRL table is searched for rows with the CRSNBR equal to MGT630 and a GRADE equal to "F." An SID of 359 is returned. Finally, the STUDENT table is searched for the student names with SIDs equal to the set of student IDs retrieved from the middle SELECT-FROM-WHERE block. (359 was the only student ID retrieved.) PELNICK is displayed.

The next example illustrates the use of a subquery that makes two passes through the same table to find the desired results.

EXAMPLE 5.6   List the names of the faculty members in the same department as PETERS. Assume that you don't know PETERS' department.

(continued on next page)

The statement

```
SELECT   FNAME, DEPT ──────────────────────   = can be used if only
FROM     FACULTY                               a single value is
WHERE    DEPT =                                returned from the
                                               subquery.
   ( SELECT   DEPT
     FROM      FACULTY
     WHERE    FNAME = 'PETERS' )
```

results in

FNAME DEPT

JARDIN FIN
PETERS FIN

The subquery searches the FACULTY table and returns the value FIN, which is PETERS' department. Then the outer SELECT block searches the FACULTY table again to retrieve all faculty members with DEPT = 'FIN'. Thus, JARDIN and PELNICK are retrieved.

YOUR TURN

5. List the name of any student receiving a grade of "A" in any course.

6. Can a subquery be used to display the student name and course number of any student receiving a grade of "A" in any course?

7. Who is teaching FIN601?

8. Write a query that displays the name, major, and grade point average for the student with the highest grade point average.

9. Which faculty members in the Accounting Department earn a salary greater than JARDIN?

10. List the student name and grade point average of any student whose GPA is above the average for the university.

11. List the major and the average GPA for all majors (not individual students) that have a GPA below the average for the university. For example, if the average GPA for the univerity is 2.8, then list the majors where the average for all students in that major is below 2.8.

12. List faculty members, including name, department, and salary, who earn more than the average salary paid to all faculty members.

13. What is the name of the faculty member with the highest salary?

14. Rewrite Example 5.5 using a join operation instead of a subquery.

15. List the faculty name, course number, and course title for any faculty member teaching more than one course.

FORMING COMPLEX QUERIES—A FINAL LOOK

***Joining a Table to Itself*

The sections of this chapter that are identified with triple asterisks (***) contain material that may be too technical for end users. These sections can be skipped without loss of continuity.

In some situations, you may find it necessary to join a table to itself, as though you were joining two separate tables. This is referred to as a **self-join.** In the self-join, the combined result consists of two rows from the same table. For example, suppose that within the FACULTY table, the head of a department is assigned the rank of "CHR." To obtain a list of faculty members that includes the name of the faculty member and the name of his or her department chair requires the use of a self-join.

To join a table to itself, the table name appears twice in the FROM clause. To distinguish between the appearance of the same table name, a temporary name, called an **alias** or a **correlation name**, is assigned to each mention of the table name in the FROM clause. The form of the FROM clause with an alias is

```
FROM  table-name [alias1] [, table-name [alias2] ] ...
```

To help clarify the meaning of the query, the alias can be used as a qualifier, in the same way that the table name serves as a qualifier, in SELECT and WHERE clauses.

EXAMPLE 5.7   As part of an analysis of the university's salary structure, you want to identify the names of any associate professors who are earning more than any full professors.

The query

```
SELECT  ASSOCIAT.FNAME, ASSOCIAT.SALARY
FROM    FACULTY  ASSOCIAT, FACULTY  FULL
WHERE   ASSOCIAT.RANK = 'ASSO' AND FULL.RANK = 'FULL'
  AND   ASSOCIAT.SALARY > FULL.SALARY
```

results in

```
FNAME     SALARY

BARGES    35000
DARDEN    37000
```

(continued on next page)

In this query, the FACULTY table, using the alias feature of SQL, is treated as two separate tables named ASSOCIAT and FULL, as shown here:

ASSOCIAT Table

FID	FNAME	EXT	DEPT	RANK	SALARY
036	BARGES	325	MGT	ASSO	35000
117	JARDIN	212	FIN	FULL	33000
098	KENNEDY	176	ACC	ASSO	30000
075	SAMPLE	171	MKT	ASST	25000
138	WARD	125	MGT	INST	20000
219	PETERS	220	FIN	FULL	45000
151	DARDEN	250	ACC	ASSO	37000
113	PIERCE	205	MGT	INST	22000

FULL Table

FID	FNAME	EXT	DEPT	RANK	SALARY
036	BARGES	325	MGT	ASSO	35000
117	JARDIN	212	FIN	FULL	33000
098	KENNEDY	176	ACC	ASSO	30000
075	SAMPLE	171	MKT	ASST	25000
138	WARD	125	MGT	INST	20000
219	PETERS	220	FIN	FULL	45000
151	DARDEN	250	ACC	ASSO	37000
113	PIERCE	205	MGT	INST	22000

The join operation is evaluated as follows:

1. Using the compound condition

ASSOCIAT.RANK = 'ASSO' AND FULL.RANK = 'FULL'

each associate professor record (BARGES, KENNEDY, DARDEN) in the AS-SOCIAT table is joined with each full professor record (JARDIN, PETERS) from the FULL table to form the following intermediate result:

ASSOCIAT Table

FID	FNAME	EXT	DEPT	RANK	SALARY
036	BARGES	325	MGT	ASSO	35000
036	BARGES	325	MGT	ASSO	35000
098	KENNEDY	176	ACC	ASSO	30000
098	KENNEDY	176	ACC	ASSO	30000
151	DARDEN	250	ACC	ASSO	37000
151	DARDEN	250	ACC	ASSO	37000

FULL Table

FID	FNAME	EXT	DEPT	RANK	SALARY
117	JARDIN	212	FIN	FULL	33000
219	PETERS	220	FIN	FULL	45000
117	JARDIN	212	FIN	FULL	33000
219	PETERS	220	FIN	FULL	45000
117	JARDIN	212	FIN	FULL	33000
219	PETERS	220	FIN	FULL	45000

Notice that every associate professor row is combined with each full professor record.

2. Using the condition

ASSOCIAT.SALARY > FULL.SALARY

for each row of the joined table, the salary value from the ASSOCIAT portion is compared with the corresponding salary value from the FULL portion. If ASSOCIAT.SALARY is greater than FULL.SALARY, then ASSOCIAT.FNAME and ASSOCIAT.SALARY are retrieved in the final table.

*** *Correlated Subqueries*

All the previous examples of subqueries evaluated the innermost query completely before moving to the next level of the query. Some queries, however, cannot be completely evaluated before the outer, or main, query is evaluated. Instead, the search condition of a subquery depends on a value in each row of the table named in the outer query. Therefore, the subquery is evaluated repeatedly, once for each row selected from the outer table. This type of subquery is referred to as a **correlated subquery.**

EXAMPLE 5.8   Retrieve the name, major, and grade point average of any student whose GPA is above the average for his or her major.

The query

```
          SELECT   POSSIBLE.SNAME, POSSIBLE.MAJOR, POSSIBLE.GPA
Main query.─────── FROM     STUDENT POSSIBLE ──────────────┐
          WHERE    GPA >                                   │
                                                   ──── Alias.
            ( SELECT   AVG(GPA)
Subquery.─────── FROM     STUDENT AVERAGE ───────────────┘
            WHERE   POSSIBLE.MAJOR = AVERAGE.MAJOR )
```

results in

SNAME	MAJOR	GPA
POIRIER	MGT	3.2
PELNICK	FIN	3.6
QUICK	MGT	3.5
ANDERSON	ACC	3.7

The column AVERAGE.MAJOR correlates with MAJOR in the main, or outer, query. In other words, the average GPA for a major is calculated in the subquery using the major of each student from the table in the main query (POSSIBLE). The subquery computes the average GPA for this major and then compares it with a row in the POSSIBLE table. If the GPA in the POSSIBLE table is greater than the average GPA for the major, the student's name, major, and GPA are displayed.

The process of the correlated subquery works in the following manner. The major of the first row in POSSIBLE (POIRIER's row) is used in the subquery to compute an average GPA. In effect, the subquery is

```
          SELECT   AVG(GPA)
          FROM     STUDENT AVERAGE
          WHERE    'MGT' = AVERAGE.MAJOR
                        └────────────────── This is the value
                                            from the first row
                                            in POSSIBLE.
```

This pass through the subquery results in a value of 2.925, the average GPA for MGT. In the outer query, POIRIER's GPA of 3.2 is compared with the average GPA for MGT; since it is greater, POIRIER's name is displayed.

This process continues; next, PARKER's row in POSSIBLE (FIN is the major) is evaluated. This time the subquery is evaluated as follows:

```
SELECT   AVG(GPA)
FROM     STUDENT AVERAGE
WHERE    'FIN' = AVERAGE.MAJOR
```

The results of this pass through the subquery is an average GPA of 3.0 for FIN. Since PARKER has a GPA of 2.7, this record is not displayed.

Every student in POSSIBLE is examined in a similar manner before this subquery is completed.

***Subquery Using EXISTS**

There may be situations in which you are interested in retrieving records where there exists at least one row that satisfies a particular condition. For example, the faculty records stored in the FACULTY table include individuals on sabbatical or leaves of absence, researchers with no teaching responsibilities, etc. If you wanted to know which faculty members had teaching duties during the current term, an existence test using the keyword EXISTS can be used to answer such a query.

This type of query is developed with a subquery. The WHERE clause of the outer query is used to test the existence of rows that result from a subquery. The form of the WHERE clause that is linked to the subquery is

```
WHERE   [NOT]   EXISTS( subquery )
```

This clause is satisfied if there is at least one row that would be returned by the subquery. If so, the subquery does not return any values; it just sets an indicator value to true. On the other hand, if no elements satisfy the condition, or the set is empty, the indicator value is false.

EXAMPLE 5.9 Retrieve a list of students currently taking courses. Assume that some students in the STUDENT table are not enrolled in any courses this term (for example, university year abroad, medical leave, working in coop program).

(continued on next page)

The query

```
SELECT   SNAME
FROM     STUDENT
WHERE    EXISTS

   ( SELECT   *
     FROM     CRSENRL
     WHERE    STUDENT.SID = CRSENRL.SID )
```

The * is used in the SELECT clause since all you want to know is if the subquery returns a row, not any particular column in a row.

results in

```
SNAME

POIRIER
PARKER
RICHARDS
PELNICK
FAGIN
MEGLIN
```

In this query, the subquery cannot be evaluated completely before the outer query is evaluated. Instead, we have a correlated subquery. For each row in STUDENT, a join of STUDENT and CRSENRL tables is performed (even though CRSENRL is the only table that appears in the subquery's FROM clause) to determine if there is a student ID in CRSENRL that matches a student ID in STUDENT.

For example, for the first row in the STUDENT table (SID = 987), the subquery evaluates as "true" if at least one row in the CRSENRL table has a SID = 987; otherwise, the expression evaluates as "false." Since there are three rows in CRSENRL with SID = 987, the expression is true and POIRIER's row is displayed. Each row in STUDENT is evaluated in a similar manner, as illustrated in Figure 5.2.

FIGURE 5.2   Interim Table in the Join between STUDENT and CRSENRL Tables

STUDENT Table   CRSENRL Table

SID	SNAME	SEX	MAJOR	GPA	CRSNBR	SID	GRADE	EXISTS (subquery)
987	POIRIER	F	MGT	3.2	MGT630	987	A	
					FIN602	987	B	TRUE
					MKT610	987	A	
763	PARKER	F	FIN	2.7	FIN601	763	B	
					FIN602	763	B	TRUE
					ACC610	763	B	

(continued on next page)

218	RICHARDS	M	ACC	2.4	ACC610	218	A	
					ACC661	218	A	TRUE
					MGT630	218	C	
359	PELNICK	F	FIN	3.6	MGT630	359	F	
					MGT681	359	B	TRUE
					MKT610	359	A	
862	FAGIN	M	MGT	2.2	MKT610	862	A	
					MKT670	862	A	TRUE
					ACC610	862	B	
748	MEGLIN	M	MGT	2.8	MGT630	748	C	
					MGT681	748	B	TRUE
					FIN601	748	A	
506	LEE	M	FIN	2.7				FALSE
581	GAMBRELL	F	MKT	3.8				FALSE
372	QUICK	F	MGT	3.5				FALSE
126	ANDERSON	M	ACC	3.7				FALSE

Often, a query is formed to test if no rows are returned in a subquery. In this case, the following form of the existence test is used:

WHERE   NOT   EXISTS(subquery)

EXAMPLE 5.10   List the faculty members who are not involved in teaching any courses this term.

The query

```
SELECT   FNAME
FROM     FACULTY
WHERE    NOT EXISTS
   ( SELECT  *
     FROM     COURSE
     WHERE    FACULTY.FID  =  COURSE.FID )
```

results in

```
FNAME

DARDEN
PIERCE
```

Again, we have an example of a correlated subquery. Figure 5.3 illustrates how each row in the FACULTY table is evaluated with the records in the COURSE table to determine which faculty members are not teaching.

FIGURE 5.3   Interim Table in the Join between FACULTY and COURSE Tables

FACULTY Table

FID	FNAME	EXT	DEPT	RANK	SALARY
036	BARGES	325	MGT	ASSO	35000
117	JARDIN	212	FIN	FULL	33000
098	KENNEDY	176	ACC	ASSO	30000
075	SAMPLE	171	MKT	ASST	25000
138	WARD	125	MGT	INST	20000
219	PETERS	220	FIN	FULL	45000
151	DARDEN	250	ACC	ASSO	37000
113	PIERCE	205	MGT	INST	22000

COURSE Table

CRSNBR	CNAME	...	FID	EXISTS	NOT EXISTS
MGT681	INTERNA	...	036	TRUE	FALSE
FIN601	MANAGER	...	117	TRUE	FALSE
ACC661	TAXATIO	...	098	TRUE	FALSE
ACC610	BASIC A	...	098		
MKT610	MKTING	...	075	TRUE	FALSE
MKT670	PRODUCT	...	075		
MGT630	INTRO T	...	138	TRUE	FALSE
FIN602	INVEST	...	219	TRUE	FALSE
				FALSE	TRUE
				FALSE	TRUE

Combining Query Results Using the UNION Operator

The UNION operator is used to merge the results of two or more queries into a single result. Each query is connected by a UNION operator to produce the result. In the process of merging the queries, duplicate rows are removed from the answer. The general form of the operator is

```
SELECT statement

UNION

SELECT statement

UNION
SELECT statement

...

[ORDER BY  integer [DESC] ]
```

COMMAND DISCUSSION

1. The system first executes each query separately; the results from each query are merged with the results of the next query, until all the queries have been merged. Any duplicate rows that occur are removed from the results.

2. In order for queries to be merged, they must be **union-compatible;** i.e., the data types and lengths of the corresponding items in each SELECT clause must be identical.

3. If ordering of the final, or merged, output is desired, the ORDER BY clause is placed after the last query only and applies to the entire result. Since the column name in each query may vary, the sort key must be specified as a number (refer to Chapter 3), not a column name.

EXAMPLE 5.11　　The Management Club has a guest speaker coming to the next meeting. The club president wants to notify students about the meeting. The president decides to notify all management majors and any students taking courses in management (i.e., both majors and nonmajors).

The statement

```
SELECT   SID
FROM     STUDENT                          Query to find students
WHERE    MAJOR = 'MGT'                     majoring in MGT.

UNION

SELECT   DISTINCT SID                      Query to find students
FROM     CRSENRL                           enrolled in MGT
WHERE    CRSNBR LIKE 'MGT%'                courses.
```

Order output by first ——— ORDER BY   1
item in SELECT clause.

results in

```
SID

218
359
372
748
862
987
```

SQL executes the top query and accesses the students majoring in management (372, 748, 862, 987). Separately, the students taking management (MGT) courses are retrieved (218, 359, 748, 987). The results are merged, and any duplicates (748, 987) are removed. Thus, six rows are output (218, 359, 372, 748, 862, 987).

This chapter concludes our look at queries. Next, you will study the remaining data manipulation commands: INSERT, UPDATE, and MODIFY.

Video Rental, Inc. Case
CHAPTER ASSIGNMENT

1. Which members (name) currently have movies rented? Write the query by using a join condition and, then again, by using a subquery.

2. a. For each member with movies currently rented, list the member name and the ID of each movie.

    b. Include the name of the movie in the output.

3. **a.** List the title of each movie and the number of times it has been rented.

    b. Order the report so that the most frequently rented movie appears first.

4. Which movies have never been rented? Display the titles.

5. Which members have rented movies on more than one occasion? Display the member's name and address.

6. What were the rental receipts for May 11, 1987?

7. For the month of May, count the number of rentals by movie category.

Chapter 6

Keeping the Database Current

To keep the data in your database current, three types of transactions must be performed on the data. These transactions are

1. Adding new records.
2. Changing existing records.
3. Deleting records no longer needed.

ADDING NEW RECORDS

Once a table has been defined and before any data can be retrieved, data must be entered into the table. Initially, data can be entered into the table in several ways:

1. Batch mode   Data is loaded into the table from a file.

2. Interactive mode   Data for each record is added by interactive prompting of each column in a record.

3. Line input   A row of data is keyed for insertion into a table using a line editor and then is submitted to the database.

Inserting One Row at a Time

In addition to initially loading data into tables, records can be added at any time to keep a table current. For example, if a new faculty member is hired, a new record, or row, should be added to the FACULTY table. In SQL, the INSERT command is used to enter a row into a table. The command has two formats:

1. Entering one row at a time.
2. Entering multiple rows at a time.

In the first format, the user enters values one row at a time, using the following version of the INSERT command:

When all columns in a table have data values assigned, this option is not used.

```
INSERT INTO table-name [ (column-name1 [,column-name2] ...)]
VALUES (value1, value2 ...)
```

COMMAND DISCUSSION

1. The INSERT INTO clause indicates that you intend to add a row to a table.

2. Following the INSERT INTO clause, the user specifies the name of the table in which the data is to be inserted.

3. When data values are being entered for all columns in the table, there is no need to list the column names following the INSERT INTO clause. However, sometimes when a row is added, only some of the column values are known at the time. In those cases, the columns being added must be listed following the table name, and only those values corresponding to the listed column names can appear following the VALUES clause. All column values of the new row that are not listed receive a NULL value.

4. Following the keyword VALUES are the values to be added to one row of a table. The entire row of values is placed within parentheses. Each data value is separated from the next by a comma. The first value corresponds to the first column in the table; the second value corresponds to the second column in the table, and so on.

EXAMPLE 6.1   When the STUDENT table is first created, it has no student data stored in it. Add the first student record to the table:

```
ID = 987
NAME = POIRIER
SEX = FEMALE
MAJOR = MANAGEMENT
GPA = 3.2
```

If you enter the command

```
INSERT INTO STUDENT
VALUES ('987','POIRIER','F','MGT',3.2)
```

Quotes are placed around character values so SQL can distinguish data values from column names.

(continued on next page)

the message displayed on the screen will be

1 Record Created

A new student record has been added to the STUDENT table. Now the table looks like this:

STUDENT Table

SID	SNAME	SEX	MAJOR	GPA
987	POIRIER	F	MGT	3.2

EXAMPLE 6.2   Let's add a second student record. Assume we have only the following data:

NAME = JONES
SEX = MALE

The statement

INSERT INTO STUDENT (SNAME,SEX)
VALUES ('JONES','M')

results in the message

Since all columns in STUDENT table are not included, the column names being added are listed following the INSERT INTO clause.

Error: Missing Mandatory Column During Insert

When the STUDENT table was defined, the student ID column included the NOT NULL keyword. (See page 15.) This means a record can be added only if the student ID is included as part of the data. Since the student ID was not included, the INSERT command was not successful.

Assume JONES's ID is 110. Now add the record.

The statement

INSERT INTO STUDENT (SID,SNAME,SEX)
VALUES ('110','JONES','M')

(continued on next page)

results in the message

1 Record Created

The STUDENT table now has the following stored values. Notice that null values are stored in the columns MAJOR and GPA, which were not included in the INSERT command.

STUDENT Table

SID	SNAME	SEX	MAJOR	GPA
987	POIRIER	F	MGT	3.2
110	JONES	M		

Null values.

Inserting Multiple Rows at One Time

In addition to adding values to a table one row at a time, you can also use a variation of the INSERT command to load some or all data from one table into another table. The second form of the INSERT command is used when you want to create a new table based on the results of a query against an existing table. The form of this INSERT command is

```
INSERT INTO  table-name
    SELECT  expression1 [ , expression2] ...
    FROM    table-name
    [WHERE  search-condition]
```

COMMAND DISCUSSION

1. The INSERT INTO clause indicates that you intend to add a row(s) to a table.

2. Following the INSERT INTO clause, the user specifies the name of the table to be updated.

3. The query is evaluated, and a copy of the results from the query is stored in the table specified after the INSERT INTO clause. If rows already exist in the table being copied to, then the new rows are added to the end of the table.

EXAMPLE 6.3   The university Dean uses a cutoff date of October 15 for preparing statistical reports on enrollments. Any reports prepared by the Dean must reflect the enrollment as of that date. The STUDENT table, however, is constantly being updated with adds, deletes, and changes. Thus, the administration decides to create a new student table that reflects student data up to and including October 15 but not thereafter.

Step 1:   Create a new table named STU_STAT.

The statement

```
CREATE TABLE  STU_STAT ─────────────────── This table is empty.
  ( SID      CHAR(3)    NOT NULL,
    SNAME    CHAR(10),
    SEX      CHAR(1),
    MAJOR    CHAR(3),
    GPA      DECIMAL(3,2) )
```

results in the message

```
Table Created
```

Step 2:   Copy the data in the STUDENT table to the STU_STAT table.

The statement

```
INSERT INTO STU_STAT
  SELECT  *
  FROM    STUDENT
```

results in the message

```
10 Records Created
```

The message "10 Records Created" indicates that the results have been copied to the new table, STU_STAT. The values in the original table, STUDENT, are still stored in the STUDENT table. Now that the new table has data values, you can query the STU_STAT table.

Any subsequent changes to the STUDENT table, such as dropouts, curriculum changes, and the like, will not appear in the STU_STAT table. So, even if a report is requested in December, enrollments as of October 15 will be reflected as long as the STU_STAT table is used to prepare the report.

YOUR TURN

1. Add a new course: FIN603, PORTFOLIO MANAGEMENT, 4 credits, maximum enrollment of 25, and taught by WARD (FID = 138).

2. LEE, whose student ID is 506, has added FIN601, but no grade has been assigned yet. Add this data to the CRSENRL table.

3. Create a TRANSCRIPT table that includes student ID, course ID, grade, and the term the course was taken. Copy the CRSENRL table to the TRANSCRIPT table.

DELETING RECORDS

Records are removed from the database when they are no longer relevant to the application. For example, if a faculty member leaves the university, data concerning that person can be removed. Deleting a record removes all data values in a row from a table. In SQL, one or more rows from a table can be deleted with the use of a DELETE command. This command has the following form:

```
DELETE FROM table-name
[WHERE search-condition]
```

COMMAND DISCUSSION

1. The DELETE FROM clause indicates you want to remove a row from a table. Following this clause, the user specifies the name of the table from which data is to be deleted.

2. To find the record(s) being deleted, use a search condition similar to that used in the SELECT statement.

EXAMPLE 6.4   A student whose ID is 106 has dropped FIN601.

The statement

```
DELETE FROM CRSENRL
WHERE CRSNBR = 'FIN601'  AND  SID = '106'
```

results in

(continued on next page)

1 Record Deleted

All records that satisfy the search condition are deleted. In this case, one record is deleted from the table.

EXAMPLE 6.5   A student whose ID number is 102 leaves the university. First delete the courses in which student 102 is enrolled.

The statement

    DELETE FROM CRSENRL
    WHERE SID = '102'

results in the message

3 Records Deleted

In this example, three records are deleted because student 102 is enrolled in three courses.

Now delete the student whose ID number is 102.

The statement

    DELETE FROM STUDENT
    WHERE SID = '102'

results in the message

1 Record Deleted

When you delete records, aim for consistency. For example, if you intend to delete MEGLIN's record in the STUDENT table, you must also delete the courses, if any, in which MEGLIN is enrolled. This involves two separate operations. Otherwise, the CRSENRL table will contain enrollment records for a student, but the STUDENT table no longer contains the student's record.

EXAMPLE 6.6   The semester is over. Remove all the courses from the current CRSENRL table.

The statement

    DELETE FROM CRSENRL

(continued on next page)

results in the message

18 Records Deleted

All the rows of the CRSENRL table have been deleted, so the table is empty. However, the definition of the table has not been deleted; it still exists even though it has no data values, so rows can be added to the table at any time.

It is important to note the difference between the DELETE command and the DROP TABLE command. In the former, you eliminate one or more rows from the indicated table. However, the structure of the table is still defined, and rows can be added to the table at any time. In the case of the DROP TABLE command, the table definition is removed from the system catalog. You have removed not only access to the data in the table but also access to the table itself. Thus, to add data to a "dropped" table, you must first create the table again.

YOUR TURN   **4.** Delete FAGIN from the STUDENT table.

UPDATING RECORDS

Very often data currently stored in a table needs to be corrected or changed. For example, a name may be misspelled or a salary figure increased. To modify the values of one or more columns in one or more records of a table, the user specifies the UPDATE command. The general form of this statement is

```
UPDATE   table-name
SET      column-name1 = expression1
         [, column-name2 = expression2] ...
[WHERE   search-condition]
```

COMMAND DISCUSSION

1. The UPDATE clause indicates which table is to be modified.

2. The SET clause is followed by the column(s) to be modified. The expression represents the new value to be assigned to the column. The expression can contain constants, NULL, column names, or arithmetic expressions. Using NULL as an expression stores a null value in the specified column.

3. The record(s) being modified is found by using a search condition. All rows that satisfy the search condition are updated. If no search condition is supplied, all rows in the table are updated.

EXAMPLE 6.7　　Change the grade of PELNICK from "B" to "A" in MGT681.

The statement

```
UPDATE  CRSENRL
SET     GRADE = 'A' ──────────────── Change being made.
WHERE   SID = '359'  AND  CRSNBR = 'MGT681'
```

results in the message

```
1 Record Updated
```

For all records that satisfy the search condition, a change is made. In this example, only one row is updated.

EXAMPLE 6.8　　All faculty members are to receive a 5 percent increase in salary.

The statement

```
UPDATE  FACULTY
SET     SALARY = SALARY * 1.05
```

results in the message

```
8 Records Updated
```

All rows in the FACULTY table are changed to reflect the salary increase. A word of caution: it's easy to "accidentally" modify all rows in a table. Check your statement carefully before executing it.

YOUR TURN

5. RICHARDS has changed from an accounting to a marketing major. Update the records in the STUDENT table.

6. Change the title of FIN602 from INVESTMENT SKILLS to INVESTMENT ANALYSIS and the maximum enrollment from 25 to 40.

7. Increase salaries to Accounting and Finance faculty members by 7 percent.

This completes the data manipulation features of SQL. In the next chapter, you will learn about views: a mechanism to limit a user's access to specific portions of a database.

Video Rental, Inc. Case
CHAPTER ASSIGNMENT

1. Add a new member as follows: 125, Bowles, 19 Sissor Lane, Narragansett, RI, 3/15/87, Annual member.

2. Add a new movie as follows: 1021, *Star Wars*, AC, G, 4/12/87, 21, I.

3. A member has just rented two movies: ALLRED has rented the movies *Back to the Future* and *Pinocchio*. Assume the date rented is 5/13/87 and the date due is 5/14/87 (one-day rental). Record this transaction.

4. On 5/12/87, SASSY returns the movie rented the previous day (Invoice 10561). Record this transaction.

5. A member's address changes: DELLA has moved to 16 Market St., Kingston, RI. Update the record.

6. A member, MCLEAVEY, has moved out of the area. Delete the record.

Chapter 7

Views

DEFINING VIEWS

In the previous chapters, queries were used to access base tables. A base table is a table defined by using the CREATE TABLE command. These tables represent the permanent tables in the database and are associated with the stored data in the database.

In addition to base tables, SQL allows users of a database to have several different ways of looking at the same database. Each of these different ways is called a **view.** A view is a derived table; that is, a table that does not physically exist, although to the user of the view, it appears to exist. Actually, the contents of a view table are derived from data in the base tables according to the definition of a view. The view may consist of a subset of the columns and/or rows from a single table. In addition, views may be more complex, involving computed values or rows and columns from several tables.

There are several reasons for creating a view:

1. You may not want every user to have access to the entire database. Even though data in a database is shared, each individual or group of users may need to access only the portion of the database that applies to their particular work. Thus, a view can be used to limit a user's access to data, since only columns or rows included in the view are accessible to users retrieving data from that view. For example, several users may have access to faculty data: the Accounting chair can retrieve data on Accounting faculty members but not on other faculty members; a Personnel clerk can retrieve data on all faculty members except for salary data; the Registrar can retrieve faculty data joined with course data. Each user is operating on a view that is derived from the FACULTY table.

2. You may want to simplify the user's perception of the database. Since a view usually contains fewer columns than the overall data and can be conceptualized as a single table rather than a collection of tables, it should be easier to work with. Thus, the user is better able to understand the data he or she is working with.

A view is defined in SQL by using the CREATE VIEW command. In defining a view, you assign a name to the view and provide a query that specifies which rows and columns will be included in the view.

The general form of this command is

```
CREATE VIEW  view-name  [(view-column-name1 [, view-column-name2] ...)]
    AS  SELECT    expression1 [, expression2] ...
        FROM      table-name1 [, table-name2] ...
        [WHERE    search-condition]
        [GROUP BY  column-name1 [, column-name2] ... ]
        [HAVING   search-condition]
```

COMMAND DISCUSSION

1. If view-column names are omitted, the names of the columns in the view are the same as the columns appearing in the SELECT clause of the view definition. If you want to rename the columns in a view, then the view-column names must be added to the view definition. In fact, view-column names must be specified for all columns in a view if any column within the view is based on a function (SUM, AVG, etc.) or on an arithmetic calculation.

2. All variations of a SELECT statement can be used to define a view. The only restriction is that the ORDER BY clause is not permitted when defining a view.

3. The creation of a view does not result in a duplicate set of stored data. Instead, the definition of a view, including the SELECT command, is saved in the system catalog (discussed in Chapter 9). When a query references the database via a view, the DBMS combines the query defining the view with the user's query to form a query that is used to access the original "base" tables where the data is stored.

4. A view is normally established by a database administrator, the individual responsible for the overall function of the database, rather than by a user. Once the view is defined, many users query the database via the view rather than the original "base" tables.

5. There may be many user views defined for the same database. Each view provides a customized structure of data for a particular user.

EXAMPLE 7.1   The secretary for the Accounting Department is one of the users who has access to the Accounting faculty IDs, names, and phone extensions. The following view is developed for the Accounting secretary.

(continued on next page)

The statement

```
CREATE VIEW  ACC_FAC
    AS  SELECT  FID, FNAME, EXT
        FROM    FACULTY
        WHERE   DEPT = 'ACC'
```

results in the message

View Created

This command creates a view named ACC_FAC with three columns (faculty ID, faculty name, and extension), which correspond to the three columns in the SELECT statement. The rows included in the view represent faculty members in the Accounting (ACC) Department. The shaded portion of the FACULTY table (Figure 7.1) indicates the data that the Accounting secretary can access. However, to the user of the view, ACC_FAC can be visualized as another table in the database (Figure 7.2).

FIGURE 7.1	FACULTY Table

FID	FNAME	EXT	DEPT	RANK	SALARY
036	BARGES	325	MGT	ASSO	35000
117	JARDIN	212	FIN	FULL	33000
098	KENNEDY	176	ACC	ASSO	30000
075	SAMPLE	171	MKT	ASST	25000
138	WARD	125	MGT	INST	20000
219	PETERS	220	FIN	FULL	45000
151	DARDEN	250	ACC	ASSO	37000
113	PIERCE	205	MGT	INST	22000

FIGURE 7.2	ACC_FAC View

FID	FNAME	EXT	
098	KENNEDY	176	**This is the subset of data that the user of the ACC_FAC table can access.**
151	DARDEN	250	

Once a view has been created, it can be queried just like any other table. For example, each September the Accounting Department secretary generates data for a faculty telephone book.

(continued on next page)

The query

```
SELECT     FNAME, EXT
FROM       ACC_FAC ──────────────────── View name.
ORDER BY   FNAME
```

results in

```
FNAME       EXT

DARDEN      250
KENNEDY     176
```

This query uses the view table ACC_FAC. Notice that only the names and extensions of Accounting faculty members are retrieved.

The next example illustrates what happens when the user attempts to access data not defined in the view.

EXAMPLE 7.2   The chair of the Accounting Department is preparing for budget meetings and asks the secretary for the total amount paid for department faculty salaries.

The query

```
SELECT   SUM(SALARY)
FROM     ACC_FAC
```

results in the message

```
Error at Line 1: Invalid Column Name ──────────── Error messages vary
                                                  from system to system.
```

Since the view does not include salary data, the query cannot be executed.

ACC_FAC is an example of a view that consists of a subset of rows and columns from a single base table. A view can also involve summary statistics as the next example illustrates.

EXAMPLE 7.3 Create a view for the Business Manager that permits the retrieval of departmental salary totals and number of faculty members without disclosing individual salaries.

The statement

Names assigned for columns in view.

```
CREATE VIEW  FAC_SUM (DEPT,SUMSAL,NBRFAC)
     AS  SELECT      DEPT, SUM(SALARY), COUNT(*)
         FROM        FACULTY
         GROUP BY    DEPT
```

results in the message

View Created

The column names used to access data from FAC_SUM are DEPT, SUMSAL, and NBRFAC. The Business Manager's view of the faculty data is as follows:

DEPT	SUMSAL	NBRFAC
ACC	67000	2
FIN	78000	2
MGT	77000	3
MKT	25000	1

The Business Manager prepares a salary summary for the university by accessing FAC_SUM.

The query

```
SELECT  DEPT, NBRFAC, SUMSAL
FROM    FAC_SUM
```

results in

DEPT	NBRFAC	SUMSAL
ACC	2	67000
FIN	2	78000
MGT	3	77000
MKT	1	25000

Note that anyone using the FAC_SUM view cannot retrieve individual faculty records. For example:

(continued on next page)

The statement

```
SELECT   DEPT, FNAME ─────────────────────┐     FNAME is not part of
FROM     FAC_SUM                           │     the FAC_SUM view.
                                           │
results in the message                     │
                                           │
Error: Invalid Column Name ────────────────┘
```

Sometimes a view, or table, is developed that consists of columns from several tables. The user visualizes the data as one table rather than several tables; this simplifies the user's perception of the data that can be accessed.

EXAMPLE 7.4   Create a view for the Registrar that enables this individual to visualize selected data from the STUDENT, CRSENRL, COURSE, and FACULTY tables as being one table. This view includes course number, course name, name of person teaching the course, student ID, and student name.

The statement

```
CREATE VIEW ROSTER
   AS  SELECT  COURSE.CRSNBR, CNAME, FNAME, STUDENT.SID, SNAME
       FROM    FACULTY, COURSE, CRSENRL, STUDENT
       WHERE   FACULTY.FID = COURSE.FID
         AND   COURSE.CRSNBR = CRSENRL.CRSNBR
         AND   CRSENRL.SID = STUDENT.SID
```

results in the message

    View Created

In this example, defining the view requires the use of the join operation to combine rows and columns from four tables.

Since no column names follow the CREATE VIEW ROSTER clause, the names of the columns in the view will be the same as in the original tables.

The Registrar mentally visualizes the ROSTER table as a single table:

CRSNBR	CNAME	FNAME	SID	SNAME
MGT630	INTRO TO MANAGEMENT	WARD	987	POIRIER
FIN602	INVESTMENT SKILLS	PETERS	987	POIRIER
MKT610	MKTING FOR MANAGERS	SAMPLE	987	POIRIER
FIN601	MANAGERIAL FINANCE	JARDIN	763	PARKER
FIN602	INVESTMENT SKILLS	PETERS	763	PARKER

(continued on next page)

ACC610	BASIC ACCOUNTING	KENNEDY	763	PARKER
ACC610	BASIC ACCOUNTING	KENNEDY	218	RICHARDS
ACC661	TAXATION	KENNEDY	218	RICHARDS
MGT630	INTRO TO MANAGEMENT	WARD	218	RICHARDS
MGT630	INTRO TO MANAGEMENT	WARD	359	PELNICK
MGT681	INTERNATIONAL MGT	BARGES	359	PELNICK
MKT610	MKTING FOR MANAGERS	SAMPLE	359	PELNICK
MKT610	MKTING FOR MANAGERS	SAMPLE	862	FAGIN
MKT670	PRODUCT MARKETING	SAMPLE	862	FAGIN
ACC610	BASIC ACCOUNTING	KENNEDY	862	FAGIN
MGT630	INTRO TO MANAGEMENT	WARD	748	MEGLIN
MGT681	INTERNATIONAL MGT	BARGES	748	MEGLIN
FIN601	MANAGERIAL FINANCE	JARDIN	748	MEGLIN

When the Registrar wants a course roster for FIN601, the following query is developed.

The statement

```
SELECT   CRSNBR, CNAME, SID, SNAME
FROM     ROSTER
WHERE    CRSNBR = 'FIN601'
```

results in

CRSNBR	CNAME	SID	SNAME
FIN601	MANAGERIAL FINANCE	763	PARKER
FIN601	MANAGERIAL FINANCE	748	MEGLIN

Compare this query to Example 5.3 on page 58 where the same query was developed using the join operation.

YOUR TURN

1. What data is displayed by the following query?

   ```
   SELECT * FROM ACC_FAC
   ```

2. Rewrite the ROSTER view in Example 7.4 so that it can be accessed with the following column names: CRSNBR, CRSNAME, FACNAME, STUID, STUNAME.

3. Set up a view that includes all columns in the COURSE table and the name of the faculty member teaching the course. Name the view SCHEDULE.

4. Retrieve from the view named SCHEDULE the course number and name for all courses taught by KENNEDY.

5. What happens if you try to retrieve an individual faculty record from FAC_SUM? (Refer to Example 7.3.)

USING A VIEW TO MODIFY A TABLE

In addition to using views to write queries, you can also use INSERT, UPDATE, and DELETE commands with views.

EXAMPLE 7.5 A faculty member, DARDEN, changes offices and receives a new phone extension. The Accounting secretary, using the view ACC_FAC, updates the phone extension. DARDEN's new extension is 943.

The statement

```
UPDATE    ACC_FAC
   SET    EXT = '943'
 WHERE    FID = '151'
```

results in the message

```
1 Record Updated
```

The change to DARDEN's row has actually been made to the base table FACULTY. However, the result of this change is now visible to users of the ACC_FAC view, the FACULTY table, and users of other views whose definition includes the column EXT.

Finally, you should be aware of some restrictions when modifying a table through a view. The use of INSERT, DELETE, and UPDATE as applied to views is not permitted under the following conditions:

1. If the view definition consists of any of the following operations: join, GROUP BY, DISTINCT, or any aggregate function. For example, the view FAC_SUM consists of columns derived from aggregate functions, so it cannot be modified; neither can the view ROSTER, which combines data from several tables.

2. If a view consists of a column derived from an expression. For example, if a view includes the column monthly salary (SALARY/12), the view cannot be modified.

DROPPING A VIEW

A view may be deleted at any time simply by using the DROP command. The general format of this command is

```
DROP VIEW view-name
```

EXAMPLE 7.6   Eliminate the view for the Accounting secretary.

The statement

    DROP VIEW ACC_FAC

results in the message

    View Dropped

Any queries that attempt to access the view ACC_FAC will no longer work since the view no longer exists.

This chapter covered the view mechanism—a way to limit a user's access to specific portions of a database. While views provide some degree of security, the granting and revoking of privileges is the primary means used in SQL to provide security. This topic will be covered in the next chapter.

Video Rental, Inc. Case
CHAPTER ASSIGNMENT

1. **a.** Prepare a view of the MOVIE table that includes the following columns: movie ID, title, movie type, rating, and status.

   b. Prepare the same view, but change the column names in the view to MID, MOVIE, TYPE, RATING, and STATUS.

2. **a.** Prepare a view combining the rental header and rental detail tables.

   b. Using the view defined in 2a, determine the total rental receipts for the month of May.

3. **a.** For all movie rentals, create a view that joins data in the RENTHEAD table (INVNBR, RENTDATE, DUEDATE, RETRNDTE), the RENTDETL table (MOVID, CHARGE), the MOVIE table (TITLE, RATING, CAT), and the MEMBER table (MEMID, MEMNAME).

   b. For all movies due to be returned on 5/12/87, use the view defined in 3a to list the movie title and the member currently renting the movie.

   c. Count the number of movies currently rented in each movie category.

Chapter 8

Security

Many people have access to a database: managers, analysts, data-entry clerks, programmers, student workers, and so on. Each individual or group needs different access to the data in the database. For example, a department chair needs to access salary data, while a telephone operator needs to access only faculty names and phone extensions.

The creation of a user view, discussed in the previous chapter, is a partial solution to the security issue: it limits the rows and columns a user can access. But it's not the whole solution. Some users only need to retrieve data, others need to update data, and still others need to update and retrieve data. Thus, including additional security features may be important to the success of database applications.

GRANTING PRIVILEGES

Many vendors of SQL products automatically make the creator of the database the administrator of security. This individual can grant to other users different powers, such as the ability to read only, to modify, or to delete data in the database. SQL, through its authorization subsystem, uses user names and passwords to control which users can see what data. Each user signs onto the computer system with his or her own user name and password (i.e., user identification) and cannot access, without permission, tables created by some other user with a different user name.

In SQL, the person who creates a table is considered the "owner" of the table. Initially, that person is the only one who can access, update, and destroy the table. The owner, however, can grant to other users the right, or privilege, to

a. access the tables or views created by the owner.
b. add, change, or delete values in a table.
c. grant rights the user receives from the owner to other users.

The owner of the table can grant to other users privileges that include the following:

- SELECT   (retrieving rows without changing values in a table)
- INSERT   (adding new rows to a table)
- UPDATE (changing values in a table)
- DELETE (removing rows from a table)
- ALTER   (modifying the definition of a table)

The authorization subsystem of SQL is based on privileges that are controlled by the statements GRANT and REVOKE. The GRANT command allows the "owner" of a table to specify the operations, or privileges, that other users may perform on a table. The format of the command is

```
GRANT  [ALL]
          privilege1 [, privilege2 ] ...
ON        table-name1/view-name1  [, table-name2/view-name2 ] ...
TO        PUBLIC
          userid1 [, userid2] ...
[WITH GRANT OPTION]
```

COMMAND DISCUSSION

1. GRANT is a required keyword that indicates you are granting access to tables or views to other users.

2. Privilege refers to the type of privilege or privileges you are granting. One or more of the following privileges can be granted: SELECT, INSERT, UPDATE, DELETE, and ALTER. Alternatively, ALL can be specified if all of the above actions are to be granted to the user.

3. ON indicates the table(s) or view(s) to which these privileges are being assigned.

4. PUBLIC is used if the privileges are to be granted to all users. If you want only certain users to have privileges assigned to this table, you must list the user identifications (userids) of all those who will be allowed to share the table.

5. If the clause WITH GRANT OPTION is specified, the recipient of the privileges specified can grant these same privileges to other users.

EXAMPLE 8.1   The Dean of Faculty, the owner of the FACULTY table, grants the SELECT privilege to the Dean of the College of Business. The owner of the table issues the following command.

The statement

```
GRANT  SELECT  ──────────────────────  Read-only access.
ON     FACULTY
TO     BUSDEAN  ──────────────────────  User ID of person
                                         being granted read-
results in the message                   only access to the
                                         FACULTY table.
```

Grant Succeeded

EXAMPLE 8.2   The owner of the FACULTY table allows the clerks in Personnel to add and modify faculty data.

The statement

```
GRANT  UPDATE, INSERT
ON     FACULTY
TO     CLERK1, CLERK2  ─────────────────  Each clerk has a
                                           different user ID.
```

results in the message

Grant Succeeded

EXAMPLE 8.3   The owner of the FACULTY table gives the Personnel Manager complete access (SELECT, INSERT, UPDATE, DELETE, ALTER) to the FACULTY table, along with permission to assign these privileges to others.

The statement

```
GRANT  ALL
ON     FACULTY
TO     PRSONMGR
WITH GRANT OPTION  ─────────────────────  Allows Personnel
                                           Manager to grant these
                                           privileges to other
results in the message                     users.
```

Grant Succeeded

EXAMPLE 8.4   The Registrar, the owner of both the STUDENT and the COURSE tables, allows all users read-only access to the COURSE table.

The statement

```
GRANT  SELECT
ON     COURSE
TO     PUBLIC
```

results in the message

```
Grant Succeeded
```

In many organizations, the owner of a table, or the person responsible for the administration of the database, will create different views of the data (discussed in Chapter 7) and then grant various users certain privileges with respect to these views. For example, a view of an employee table can be defined so that it excludes salaries. Another view might provide only summary salary data by department or job classification. The authorization subsystem of SQL ensures that access to these views is given only to users specifically authorized to use the views.

EXAMPLE 8.5   The Student Association president is given read-only access to a view of the STUDENT table that includes the student's name, ID, major, and sex.

Step 1:

The statement

```
CREATE VIEW STUNT_AS ─────────────────────  View is created by
    AS  SELECT  SID, SNAME, MAJOR, SEX         owner of STUDENT
        FROM    STUDENT                         table.
```

results in the message

```
View Created
```

Step 2:

The statement

```
GRANT  SELECT ──────────────────────────  Read-only access to
ON     STUNT_AS                              the view is granted.
TO     PRES
```

(continued on next page)

results in the message

Grant Succeeded

EXAMPLE 8.6   The class president, who was granted read-only access to the STUNT_AS table, wants a list of all student names and majors.

The statement

```
SELECT   SNAME, MAJOR
FROM     REGISTRA.STUNT_AS
```

results in

User ID of the owner of a table is normally required as a prefix to the table name in order to access a table owned by someone else.

SNAME	MAJOR
POIRIER	MGT
PARKER	FIN
RICHARDS	ACC
PELNICK	FIN
FAGIN	MGT
MEGLIN	MGT
LEE	FIN
GAMBRELL	MKT
QUICK	MGT
ANDERSON	ACC

In order for you to access a table "owned" by someone else (assuming you have been granted permission), you must prefix the table being accessed in the FROM clause with the "owner's" user ID.

EXAMPLE 8.7   The class president wants to see the courses in which QUICK, SID = 372, is enrolled.

The query

```
SELECT   SID, CRSNBR
FROM     REGISTRA.CRSENRL
WHERE    SID = '372'
```

results in the message

Table or View Does Not Exist

Error message is displayed. The class president hasn't been granted access to the CRSENRL table.

YOUR TURN	**1.** Give the class president read-only rights to the STUDENT and CRSENRL tables. (Userid is PRES.)
	2. The Personnel Manager creates a view named CLERKVW that contains all faculty data except salaries. Assign the data-entry clerks read-only privileges. (Userid is CLERK.)
	3. Give ARDEN and FRANCO update rights to the STUDENT table.
	4. Give all users all privileges to the COURSE table.

REMOVING PRIVILEGES

Privileges assigned to other users can be taken away by the person who granted them. In SQL, the REVOKE statement is used to remove privileges granted by the GRANT command. The general form of this statement is

```
REVOKE   [ALL]
         privilege1 [, privilege2 ] ...
ON       table-name1/view-name1 [, table-name2/view-name2 ] ...
FROM     PUBLIC
         userid1 [, userid2] ...
```

COMMAND DISCUSSION

1. REVOKE is a required keyword that indicates you are removing access to tables or views.

2. Privilege refers to the type of privilege or privileges you are revoking. One or more of the following privileges can be revoked: SELECT, INSERT, UPDATE, DELETE, and ALTER. Alternatively, ALL can be specified if all of the above actions are to be taken away from the user.

3. The ON clause indicates the table(s) or view(s) from which these privileges are being removed.

4. PUBLIC is used if the privileges are taken away from all users of the indicated table(s). Otherwise, you list the user names of only those who are no longer allowed to share the table.

EXAMPLE 8.8   The Personnel clerks no longer need to access the FACULTY table. Revoke their privileges.

The statement

```
REVOKE    UPDATE, INSERT
ON        FACULTY
FROM      CLERK1, CLERK2
```

results in the message

```
Revoke Succeeded
```

YOUR TURN   **5.** Remove access to the COURSE table that was given to all users.

This completes the discussion of security features in SQL. In the next chapter, you will be introduced to several other administrative features that can be implemented in SQL.

Video Rental, Inc. Case
CHAPTER ASSIGNMENT

1. Allow the assistant manager (ASSTMGR) to update and read all the tables in the database.

2. The store manager is to be given read, insert, and delete privileges on all tables. The manager's userid is MANAGER.

3. Allow the clerk to read the MOVIE table. The clerk's userid is CLERK.

Chapter 9

Administration of the Database

This chapter covers several topics related to the administration of the database. These topics include the following:

- Accessing information about the database by using SQL's system catalog.
- Modifying the structure of a table by using the ALTER command.
- Improving the performance of queries by creating indexes.

SYSTEM CATALOG

In SQL, information about the database, such as the names of tables, views, indexes, and columns, is maintained within a set of tables referred to as the *system catalog*. SQL automatically maintains these tables in the system catalog in response to commands issued by users. For example, the catalog tables are updated automatically when a new table is defined using the CREATE TABLE command.

Database administrators and end users can access data in the system catalog just as they access data in other SQL tables by using the SELECT statement. This enables a user to inquire about data in the database and serves as a useful reference tool when developing queries.

Different SQL implementations have slight variations in the set of tables and features available in their system catalogs. Table 9.1 lists the tables that make up the system catalog for the XDB implementation of SQL. Check your reference manual to review the features of the system catalog available on your system.

One commonly referenced table, SYSTABLE, contains a row for each table or view that has been defined. For each table, the following information is maintained: name of the table (NAME), authorized ID of the user who created the table (CREATOR), and type of table (TYPE). When users access SYSTABLE, they see data pertaining to tables and views that they can access.

TABLE 9.1	Overview of System Catalog Tables in XDB	
	Table Name	**Description**
	SYSAUTH	Records the privileges held by database users.
	SYSCOLS	Contains information on the columns in all database tables.
	SYSINDEX	Contains information on indexes.
	SYSKEYS	Contains one row for each column of an index key.
	SYSTABLE	Contains one row for each table or view in the database.
	SYSVIEWS	Contains the view definition.
	SYSSYN	Contains user-defined synonyms for table and view names.

EXAMPLE 9.1   Provide a list of all tables and views in the database.

The statement

```
SELECT   NAME, TYPE
FROM     SYSTABLE
```

results in

```
NAME          TYPE

STUDENT       T
FACULTY       T
COURSE        T
CRSENRL       T
ROSTER        V
FAC_SUM       V
ACC_FAC       V
```

The table SYSCOLS contains a row for every column of every table or view in the database. For each column, the following information is maintained: column name (NAME), name of the table of which the column is a part (TBNAME), data type of the column (COLTYPE), length of each column (LENGTH), position of the column in the table (COLNO), and whether NULL is permitted in the column (NULLS). Users querying SYSCOLS can retrieve data on columns in tables to which they have access.

EXAMPLE 9.2   A user wants to obtain data about students majoring in finance but doesn't know any of the column names in the STUDENT table. (Assume the user knows there is a table named STUDENT.)

(continued on next page)

The statement

```
SELECT   NAME
FROM     SYSCOLS
WHERE    TBNAME = 'STUDENT'
```

results in

NAME

SID
SNAME
SEX
MAJOR
GPA

YOUR TURN   Use the system catalog to find out the following:

1. What columns are available in the COURSE table?

2. What are the names of the views that have been defined?

MODIFYING THE DATABASE DEFINITION

As you work with the data, you may find that changes to the database are necessary. For example, you may want to enlarge a name column from 10 to 15 characters or add a building location column to the FACULTY table. Revision is the process of changing the structure of the database once the database has been established.

Unfortunately, the revision capabilities in SQL are limited and vary depending on the implementation you're using. The only change that all implementations consistently permit is to add new columns to the right of all the other columns in an existing table. The ALTER TABLE command is used to revise a table in SQL. The format of this command is

```
ALTER TABLE table-name
     ADD column-name data-type
```

COMMAND DISCUSSION

1. The ALTER TABLE clause identifies the table you intend to modify.

2. Following the keyword ADD is the column name and data type that is to be added to the table.

3. The ALTER TABLE statement may contain only one ADD clause.

EXAMPLE 9.3   Add a faculty advisor column to the STUDENT table.

The statement

```
ALTER TABLE STUDENT
    ADD FID CHAR(3)
```

results in the message

```
Table Altered
```

The STUDENT table now looks like this:

SID	SNAME	SEX	MAJOR	GPA	FID
987	POIRIER	F	MGT	3.2	
763	PARKER	F	FIN	2.7	
218	RICHARDS	M	ACC	2.4	
359	PELNICK	F	FIN	3.6	
862	FAGIN	M	MGT	2.2	
748	MEGLIN	M	MGT	2.8	
506	LEE	M	FIN	2.7	
581	GAMBRELL	F	MKT	3.8	
372	QUICK	F	MGT	3.5	
126	ANDERSON	M	ACC	3.7	

———— **The new column, FID, now exists, but no data values are stored in it. They are assigned NULL value.**

If the type of changes to a table involve deleting columns, rearranging columns, inserting columns within the table, or modifying a column's size, on most systems you must first create a new table and then load data into the new table from the existing table by using the INSERT command (format 2) discussed in Chapter 6.

EXAMPLE 9.4   After using the STUDENT table for some time, you decide the table needs to be modified. Add a new column, first name (FNAME), ahead of the SNAME column. Expand the SNAME column to 15 characters, and rename it LNAME for last name.

(continued on next page)

Step 1: Create a new table with the revised columns.

The statement

```
CREATE TABLE STUDENT2 ───────────────── New table name.
   ( SID      CHAR(3) ,
     FNAME    CHAR(10),
     LNAME    CHAR(15),
     SEX      CHAR(1),
     MAJOR    CHAR(3),
     GPA      DECIMAL(3,2) )
```

results in the message

    Table Created

The STUDENT2 table contains six columns: SID, FNAME, LNAME, SEX, **MAJOR**, and GPA.

Step 2: The next step is to load the existing student data into the new **table** (STUDENT2).

The statement

```
INSERT INTO   STUDENT2(SID,LNAME,SEX,MAJOR,GPA)
SELECT        SID, SNAME, SEX, MAJOR, GPA
FROM          STUDENT
```

results in the message

    10 Records Created

The STUDENT2 table now looks like this:

                                                    ──────── Null values for **FNAME.**

SID	FNAME	LNAME	SEX	MAJOR	GPA
987		POIRIER	F	MGT	3.2
763		PARKER	F	FIN	2.7
218		RICHARDS	M	ACC	2.4
359		PELNICK	F	FIN	3.6
862		FAGIN	M	MGT	2.2
748		MEGLIN	M	MGT	2.8
506		LEE	M	FIN	2.7
581		GAMBRELL	F	MKT	3.8
372		QUICK	F	MGT	3.5
126		ANDERSON	M	ACC	3.7

3. Add a new column "Date hired" as the last column in the FACULTY table.

4. The grading system is changed to allow plus and minus grades (C+, A-, etc.) to be stored. Modify the CRSENRL table so that the new grading system can be accommodated. The grades currently stored in CRSENRL will be copied without change (i.e., an "A" is an "A," a "B" is a "B," etc.).

5. What happens to the system catalog after the changes in the previous two exercises are made?

INDEXES

Performance

The use of indexes is one of the major ways in which the performance of queries (i.e., the speed with which results are retrieved) can be improved in relational databases. Indexes allow the DBMS to retrieve rows from a table without scanning the entire table.

A table can have one or more indexes defined for it. Each index is based on one or more columns of a table. The CREATE INDEX command is used to establish an index. The form of this command is

```
CREATE INDEX  index-name
ON   table-name
        ( column-name1 [DESC]  [,column-name2 [DESC] ] ... )
```

COMMAND DISCUSSION

1. Each index is assigned a name and is related to a particular table based on the ON table-name clause.

2. The entries in an index are ordered on one or more columns within the specified table. The index can be arranged in ascending or descending order. If descending order is desired, DESC is specified following the column name. If no order is specified, then ascending order will be used. The term **index key** refers to the set of columns in a table that is used to determine the order of entries in an index.

3. When an index consists of multiple columns, place the most important column first.

4. A table can have many different indexes associated with its columns. Each index is created by issuing a separate CREATE INDEX command.

Once an index is created, neither an end user nor an application programmer can reference the index in a query. Indexes are used automatically by the SQL system when needed to choose the best path to the data. In addition, once an index is created, it is updated automatically as rows are added or deleted from the table. Thus, the index is always current with the data in the table.

Finally, the creation of indexes improves the performance associated with processing large tables. However, an excessive number of indexes can result in an increase in processing time during update operations because of the additional effort needed to maintain the indexes. Thus, for tables undergoing frequent change, there is a "cost" associated with an excessive number of indexes. In addition, as the number of indexes increases, the storage requirements needed to hold the indexes becomes significant.

EXAMPLE 9.5

Many queries to the STUDENT table reference the student's major; therefore, the database designer decides to create an index using the MAJOR column to improve performance related to these queries.

The command

```
CREATE INDEX MAJORIND ──────────── Index name.
ON   STUDENT
     ( MAJOR ) ─────────────────── Index key.
```

results in the message

```
Index Created
```

This command creates an index named MAJORIND using the MAJOR column within the STUDENT table. The index can be used by the system to provide quick access to student data that are subject to conditions related to the student's major.

Primary Key

The primary key is an important concept in data processing. The primary key is a field or fields in a record that allows you to uniquely identify a record from all the other records in a table. For example, companies assign IDs to employees as unique identifiers. Thus, an employee ID can serve as a primary key for personnel records.

When a table is created in SQL, duplicate records can be stored in the table. The uniqueness characteristic is not enforced automatically. To prevent duplicate records from being stored in a table, a separate file called an "index" must be created. An index is created so that the DBMS can ensure that all values in a special column or columns of a table are unique. For example, the STUDENT table can be indexed on SID so that each row of the STUDENT table contains a different student ID value (i.e., no duplicate SIDs can be entered).

In addition to defining an index, the column or columns that represent the primary key should be designated as NOT NULL during the CREATE TABLE definition. The NOT NULL keyword prevents unknown values from being stored in the column that you want as the primary key. The combination of a unique index and the NOT NULL specification is necessary to define a primary key in SQL.

A variation of the CREATE INDEX command, CREATE UNIQUE INDEX, is used to establish an index that assures no duplicate primary key values are stored in a table. The form of this command is

```
CREATE [UNIQUE] INDEX index-name
ON table-name
    ( column-name1 [DESC] [, column-name2 [DESC] ] ... )
```

COMMAND DISCUSSION

1. The keyword UNIQUE in the the clause CREATE UNIQUE INDEX specifies that in the creation and maintenance of the index no two records in the index table can have the same value for the index column or column combination. Thus, any INSERT or UPDATE command that attempts to add a duplicate row in the index would be rejected.

2. Each index is assigned a name and is related to a particular table based on the ON table-name clause.

3. An index is based on one or more columns within the specified table. The index can be arranged in ascending or descending order. If you don't specify an order, then ascending order is assumed.

EXAMPLE 9.6 Create an index for the STUDENT table that prevents records with the same student ID from being stored in the table.

(continued on next page)

The command

```
CREATE  UNIQUE  INDEX   STUINDEX ──────────── Index name.
ON  STUDENT
    ( SID ) ─────────────────────────────── Index key.
```

results in the message

Index Created

An index named STUINDEX has been created on the STUDENT table for the student ID.

The index is stored separately from the STUDENT table. Figure 9.1 shows the relationship between STUDENT and STUINDEX after ten students have been added to the STUDENT table. Each row of the index, STUINDEX, consists of a column value for the index column and a pointer, or physical address, to the location of a row in the STUDENT table. As students are added or deleted from the STUDENT table, SQL automatically updates the index.

FIGURE 9.1	Relationship between STUDENT and STUINDEX

STUINDEX   STUDENT Table
Index

Pointer to a row in the table. (Not all pointers are shown.)

	SID	SNAME	SEX	MAJOR	GPA
126	987	POIRIER	F	MGT	3.2
218	763	PARKER	F	FIN	2.7
359	218	RICHARDS	M	ACC	2.4
372	359	PELNICK	F	FIN	3.6
506	862	FAGIN	M	MGT	2.2
581	748	MEGLIN	M	MGT	2.8
748	506	LEE	M	FIN	2.7
763	581	GAMBRELL	F	MKT	3.8
862	372	QUICK	F	MGT	3.5
987	126	ANDERSON	M	ACC	3.7

To conceptualize how the index works, assume you didn't realize LEE's record was already stored in the STUDENT table and you attempt to add LEE's record again.

You enter the command

```
INSERT INTO STUDENT
VALUES ('506','LEE','M','FIN',2.7)
```

(continued on next page)

and the computer responds with the message

Error: Duplicate Value in Index

This message occurs because the value 506 is already stored in STUINDEX and attempting to add another 506 value results in a duplicate value, which is not permitted in a unique index.

Now, let's add a new student named MILLER with an SID equal to 295.

You enter the command

```
INSERT INTO  STUDENT
VALUES ('295','MILLER','F','FIN',3.1)
```

and the computer responds with the message

1 Record Created

After MILLER's record is added, STUINDEX and STUDENT appear as follows:

STUINDEX Index	STUDENT Table				
	SID	SNAME	SEX	MAJOR	GPA
126	987	POIRIER	F	MGT	3.2
218	763	PARKER	F	FIN	2.7
295	218	RICHARDS	M	ACC	2.4
359	359	PELNICK	F	FIN	3.6
372	862	FAGIN	M	MGT	2.2
506	748	MEGLIN	M	MGT	2.8
581	506	LEE	M	FIN	2.7
748	581	GAMBRELL	F	MKT	3.8
763	372	QUICK	F	MGT	3.5
862	126	ANDERSON	M	ACC	3.7
987	295	MILLER	F	FIN	3.1

YOUR TURN

6. The primary key for the CRSENRL table is the combination of student ID (SID) and course number (CRSNBR). Create an index (CRENRIND) that prevents duplicate course enrollments from occurring.

Dropping an Index

Indexes, unique and nonunique, can be eliminated if they are no longer needed. The DROP INDEX command is used to remove an index. The format of this command is

```
DROP INDEX index-name
```

EXAMPLE 9.7   The index STUINDEX is no longer needed. Delete it.

The statement

    DROP INDEX STUINDEX

results in

    Index Dropped

This concludes the discussion of administrative features available in SQL. Up to this point, SQL has been viewed from the standpoint of an interactive query language. In the final chapter, we focus on SQL as an application programming language, where professional programmers can develop applications in conventional programming languages such as COBOL, FORTRAN, and PL-1.

Video Rental, Inc. Case
CHAPTER ASSIGNMENT

1. Add a new field "Year movie released" as the last column in the MOVIE table. Use RELDATE as the column name and DATE as the data type.

2. Add a zipcode column to the MEMBER table immediately after the city/state column.

3. **a.** Create a primary key for the RENTHEAD table.
   b. Create a primary key for RENTDETL table.

4. Many queries are based on movie category codes. Create an index that will increase the system's performance when queries access the MOVIE table based on movie category data.

5. Use the system catalog to identify the column names in the MOVIE table.

Chapter 10

***Embedded SQL**

Note that this chapter is identified with triple asterisks (***). It contains material that may be too technical for end users and can be skipped without loss of continuity.

SQL is used both as an interactive query language and as an application programming language. Up to now, we have focused on interactive SQL. In this chapter, we examine the development of application programs written in a host language such as COBOL, PL-1, or FORTRAN. These application programs contain SQL statements along with the standard statements of the host language. When SQL statements are included within an application program, the SQL statements are referred to as **embedded SQL.**

There are many situations when embedded SQL is more appropriate than interactive SQL. For instance:

- On-line processing of transactions involves formatted screens to more easily enter data and data validation routines to ensure the integrity of the database. Neither of these functions are possible in interactive SQL.

- Many applications are best processed in batches. Data are collected and stored until a large number of transactions accumulate or a designated time occurs. The computer processing of batch applications involves a series of runs. Each run performs one or more processing steps. Typical applications include payroll systems, cash receipts and disbursements, and general ledger. These applications are normally developed using a host language.

In principle, any SQL statement can be embedded within the host language. However, the data manipulation statements (SELECT, INSERT, UPDATE, and DELETE) are the statements most frequently used. In this chapter, we illustrate the use of embedded SQL using COBOL as the host language.

EMBEDDED SQL: RETRIEVING ONE ROW

The approach for developing application programs with embedded SQL varies depending on whether your program retrieves one row or multiple rows from the database. First, we discuss the approach followed when only one row is retrieved from the database.

In interactive SQL, when you want information on a specific student, you identify the specific student ID in the WHERE clause and write the query

```
SELECT   SNAME, MAJOR, GPA
FROM     STUDENT
WHERE    SID = '218'
```

which results in

SNAME	MAJOR	GPA
RICHARDS	ACC	2.4

Sometimes, however, it's too time-consuming or difficult for the end user to develop a query to access student data from the database. In this case, it's simpler for an application programmer to write a program containing embedded SQL statements that the end user accesses to retrieve the desired information. The user accesses the program, enters the requested student ID, and reviews the results at a terminal.

Embedded SQL statements have essentially the same syntax as the interactive SQL statements covered in the previous chapters. However, there are some variations. For instance, in order for a COBOL program to manipulate data from the database, the values retrieved from the database must be placed into variables that the COBOL program can reference.

For example, an embedded SQL query similar to the interactive query above has the following appearance:

Identifies beginning and ending of statement.

```
EXEC SQL
    SELECT   SNAME, MAJOR, GPA
    INTO     :HSNAME, :HMAJOR, :HGPA
    FROM     STUDENT
    WHERE    SID  = :HSID
END-EXEC.
```

Data retrieved from database is stored in these variables.

The ID of the specific student (perhaps SID=126) previously stored in the variable HSID.

While this SQL statement achieves the same results as the interactive version, there are some important differences:

1. Every SQL statement embedded within a COBOL program has the following structure:

```
EXEC SQL
    SQL statement
END-EXEC.
```

The keywords EXEC SQL are placed before each SQL statement and END-EXEC follows each statement. However, the period at the end of END-EXEC can be omitted within a COBOL IF statement. The keywords enable the precompiler (to be discussed in a later section) to determine when an SQL statement begins and ends. By the way, these statements are placed anywhere in columns 12 through 72.

2. The INTO clause must follow the SELECT clause in order to provide an area where the values from the database are available for manipulation by the COBOL program. The variables following the INTO clause are referred to as host variables. Host variables are defined in the WORKING-STORAGE SECTION of your COBOL program.

Figure 10.1 illustrates the structure of a COBOL program when one record, or row, is retrieved from the database. Differences from standard COBOL occur in the WORKING-STORAGE SECTION and in the PROCEDURE DIVISION. The shaded areas in the figure identify these differences. In the WORKING-STORAGE SECTION, the following memory areas must be defined:

1. host variables
2. SQL tables
3. communication area

and, in the PROCEDURE DIVISION, you must

4. code the SQL query.
5. check whether the SQL query was successfully executed.

FIGURE 10.1 Structure of a COBOL Program When a Single Row Is Retrieved

```
                    IDENTIFICATION DIVISION.

                       .  standard COBOL entries
                       .


                    ENVIRONMENT DIVISION.

                       .  standard COBOL entries
                       .


                    DATA DIVISION.
                    FILE SECTION.

                       .  standard COBOL entries
                       .
```

(continued on next page)

```
                    WORKING-STORAGE SECTION.
                      .
                      .  standard COBOL entries
                      .
```

```
                    define host variables

                    declare SQL tables

                    establish communication area (SQLCA)
```

```
                    PROCEDURE DIVISION.
                      .
                      .  standard COBOL statements
                      .
```

```
                    SQL query expression

                    error check of SQL statement
```

Host Variables

A **host variable** is a data item declared in the host language, COBOL, for use within SQL statements embedded within an application program. This is the way SQL interacts with the host language program. For example, in the statement

```
    SELECT   SNAME, GPA, MAJOR
    INTO     :HSNAME, :HGPA, :HMAJOR          Host variables are
    FROM     STUDENT          └───────────── preceded by a colon.
    WHERE    SID = :HSID
```

the host variables are HSNAME, HGPA, HMAJOR, and HSID. The host variable, when included in an SQL statement, must be preceded by a colon (:) to distinguish the host variable from SQL column names. By the way, it is permissible for host variables and column names to have the same name. When the host variable is used in a COBOL statement, as compared to an SQL statement, it is not preceded by a colon.

All host variables must be declared in the WORKING-STORAGE SECTION before being referenced in the PROCEDURE DIVISION. On some implementations, the definition of host variables is preceded by the keywords

    EXEC SQL BEGIN DECLARE SECTION END-EXEC.

and are terminated by the keywords

    EXEC SQL END DECLARE SECTION END-EXEC.

The four host variables in the above SELECT statement are declared in the WORKING-STORAGE SECTION of your COBOL program as follows:

```
WORKING-STORAGE SECTION.

    EXEC SQL  BEGIN DECLARE SECTION  END-EXEC.

01  HSNAME   PIC   X(10).
01  HGPA     PIC   9V99.
01  HMAJOR   PIC   XXX.
01. HSID     PIC   XXX.

    EXEC SQL  END DECLARE SECTION   END-EXEC.
```

DECLARE TABLE Statement

On some implementations, the SQL table or view accessed in your COBOL program can be declared in the WORKING-STORAGE SECTION using the DECLARE TABLE statement. This statement has the following format:

```
EXEC SQL
    DECLARE  table-name or view-name  TABLE
      ( column-name1 data-type [NOT NULL ]
      [,column-name2 data-type [NOT NULL ] ] ...)
END-EXEC.
```

COMMAND DISCUSSION

1. The inclusion of the table or view definition helps document the program by describing the table or view used in this program.

2. The declaration of the table enables the precompiler to perform checks that ensure SQL column names used within the program are correct.

3. This statement can be written into your program, as this example shows:

```
EXEC SQL
    DECLARE STUDENT TABLE
        ( SID      CHAR(3)  NOT NULL,
          SNAME   CHAR(10),
          SEX      CHAR(1),
          MAJOR   CHAR(3),
          GPA      DECIMAL(3,2) )
END-EXEC.
```

Communication Area

After each SQL statement is executed, the DBMS provides feedback on whether the statement worked properly. This information is returned, via a collection of variables, to an area of primary memory that is shared by the COBOL program and the SQL DBMS. This area is called the **SQL communication area (SQLCA).**

Within SQLCA, one variable, named SQLCODE, stores a value indicating the success or failure of the SQL statement just executed. An SQLCODE value of 0 means the SQL statement executed successfully. SQLCODE values greater than 0 indicate that the statement executed normally and some special condition occurred. For example, a code of 100 means end-of-data has been reached. A negative value indicates an abnormal condition has occurred and the statement did not execute successfully. For example, a system failure or no room in the database to add a record can result in a negative value stored in SQLCODE. If an abnormal condition occurs, your program should print an error message and then stop processing.

In order to provide error-checking capability, the SQL communication area must be brought into your program. To do so, code the following information into the WORKING-STORAGE SECTION of your program:

```
EXEC SQL
    INCLUDE SQLCA
END-EXEC.
```

When you preprocess your program, the SQL compiler inserts the SQLCA variables in place of the INCLUDE SQLCA statement. SQLCODE is one of these variables.

Retrieving Data

To retrieve a single row of data from the database, a SELECT statement representing the query is placed in the PROCEDURE DIVISION of your COBOL program. The SELECT statement is essentially the same as in interactive SQL, except here the statement must include an INTO clause. This additional clause allows the DBMS to put the retrieved data values, from only one row, into the program's host variables. This version of the SELECT statement has the following format:

```
EXEC SQL
    SELECT    column-name1 [, column-name2] ...
    INTO      host-variable1 [, host-variable2] ...
    FROM      table-name
    [WHERE    search-condition ]
END-EXEC.
```

COMMAND DISCUSSION

1. This version of the "embedded" SELECT statement can be used only if zero rows or one row is retrieved as a result of the execution of the statement. If more than one row is retrieved, the execution of the statement fails and SQLCODE contains a negative value.

2. The INTO clause specifies where you want the retrieved data to be stored. The data items, or host variables, following the INTO clause correspond one for one with the column names in the SELECT clause.

For example, to retrieve data on an individual student, you could incorporate the following SELECT statement within your COBOL program:

```
EXEC SQL
    SELECT   SNAME, GPA, MAJOR
    INTO     :HSNAME, :HGPA, :HMAJOR
    FROM     STUDENT
    WHERE    SID = :HSID
END-EXEC.
```

The INTO clause identifies the host variables (HSNAME, HGPA, HMAJOR) used to receive the values retrieved by the SELECT statement.

The WHERE clause uses the host variable HSID to identify the specific student row to be retrieved from the STUDENT table. Notice that HSID is declared along with the other host variables in the WORKING-STORAGE SECTION of your program. However, the value of HSID must be known before the SELECT statement is executed.

A Complete Program

A complete COBOL program displaying data for a specific student is illustrated in Figure 10.2

FIGURE 10.2   COBOL Program Illustrating Retrieval of One Row from Database

```
IDENTIFICATION DIVISION.
PROGRAM-ID. STUDENT.

ENVIRONMENT DIVISION.

DATA DIVISION.
WORKING-STORAGE SECTION.

01   OUTGPA   PIC   9.99.
```

(continued on next page)

```
1          EXEC SQL  BEGIN DECLARE SECTION  END-EXEC.

    01  HSID      PIC  999.
    01  HSNAME    PIC  X(15).                            Establishes host
    01  HMAJOR    PIC  XXX.                              variables used in
    01  HSEX      PIC  X.                                SQL statements.
    01  HGPA      PIC  9V99.

           EXEC SQL  END DECLARE SECTION   END-EXEC.     All SQL statements
                                                         must be placed in col-
2          EXEC SQL                                      umns 12 through 72.
              DECLARE STUDENT TABLE
                 ( SID      CHAR(3)  NOT NULL,
                   SNAME    CHAR(10),
                   SEX      CHAR(1),
                   MAJOR    CHAR(3),
                   GPA      DECIMAL(3,2) )
           END-EXEC.

3          EXEC SQL
              INCLUDE SQLCA
           END-EXEC.

    PROCEDURE DIVISION.

    A000-MAIN.
           PERFORM B010-GETID.
           PERFORM B020-SQL-EXECUTION.
           PERFORM B030-OUTPUT.
           STOP RUN.

    B010-GETID.

           DISPLAY  'Enter Student ID: '.
           ACCEPT HSID.

    B020-SQL-EXECUTION.

4          EXEC SQL
              SELECT   SNAME, GPA, MAJOR, SEX
              INTO     :HSNAME, :HGPA, :HMAJOR, :HSEX
              FROM     STUDENT
              WHERE    SID = :HSID
           END-EXEC.

    B030-OUTPUT.

5          IF SQLCODE = 0
              MOVE HGPA TO OUTGPA
              DISPLAY
              DISPLAY ' NAME    :  ', HSNAME
              DISPLAY ' SEX     :  ', HSEX
              DISPLAY ' MAJOR   :  ', HMAJOR
              DISPLAY ' GPA     :  ', OUTGPA
           ELSE
              PERFORM CO10-ERROR.
```

(continued on next page)

```
C010-ERROR.

    DISPLAY.
    DISPLAY ' ERROR — CODE IS : ', SQLCODE.
```

Sample output:

```
Enter Student ID: 218

    NAME    :  RICHARDS
    SEX     :  M
    MAJOR   :  ACC
    GPA     :  2.4
```

The following points refer to sections in the program that are numbered on the left:

1. The host variables are defined.

2. The SQL STUDENT table is declared.

3. The communication area is declared.

4. The student's record is retrieved from the database and moved into the host variables HSNAME, HGPA, and HMAJOR.

5. To detect whether the SQL statement executed successfully, the data item SQLCODE is checked for a value of 0. (A code of 0 indicates a successful completion.) If the SQL statement executed successfully, the program displays the output. If not, the program branches to an error routine where the value of SQLCODE is displayed.

YOUR TURN

1. Modify the program to handle the situation where a user enters an incorrect student ID number. The program in Figure 10.1 should display the message "No student found for this ID." (Hint: Use SQLCODE to test for this situation.)

EMBEDDED SQL: RETRIEVING MULTIPLE ROWS

What if you wanted to retrieve any number of rows of data from the database? For example, suppose you want to retrieve the names and grade point averages of all students majoring in management (MGT). In interactive SQL, you write the query

```
SELECT  SNAME, GPA
FROM    STUDENT
WHERE   MAJOR = 'MGT'
```

which results in

SNAME	GPA
POIRIER	3.2
FAGIN	2.2
MEGLIN	2.8
QUICK	3.5

Note that four rows are retrieved by this query.

When using embedded SQL, problems occur in situations where your application program retrieves a set of rows (more than one row) rather than a single row. Because COBOL processes records one at a time and SQL retrieves a set of records at a time, you must use a different strategy to retrieve more than one row in embedded SQL. A special data structure, called a **cursor structure,** is established in the application program to link COBOL's record-at-a-time approach with SQL's set-at-a-time approach. The cursor acts as a pointer to a specific row position within the set of rows of the cursor structure. The COBOL program uses the cursor to retrieve records one at a time.

To use a cursor in your program, you follow these steps:

1. Declare the cursor structure.

2. Open the cursor.

3. Retrieve the records one at a time from the cursor structure by using a loop structure.

4. Close the cursor.

Figure 10.3 illustrates the necessary framework of a COBOL program when retrieving more than one row from the database. The shaded areas in the figure identify the new concepts needed in your COBOL program when incorporating the cursor structure. Note that the host variables, declaring tables, and communication area are still used in your program.

FIGURE 10.3 Framework of a COBOL Program with Cursor Structure

IDENTIFICATION DIVISION.

.
. standard COBOL entries
.

ENVIRONMENT DIVISION.

.
. standard COBOL entries
.

(continued on next page)

```
DATA DIVISION.
FILE SECTION.

    .  standard COBOL entries
    .

WORKING-STORAGE SECTION.

    .  standard COBOL entries
    .

define host variables

declare SQL tables

establish communication area (SQLCA)

define cursor structure

PROCEDURE DIVISION.

    .  standard COBOL statements
    .

OPEN cursor

FETCH a record

error check of SQL statement

CLOSE cursor
```

Cursor Structure

The cursor structure represents an area in memory allocated for temporarily storing and processing the results of an SQL SELECT statement from within a COBOL program.

A cursor structure is defined by a DECLARE CURSOR statement. This statement assigns a name to the results of a query (the SQL SELECT statement) that is part of the cursor definition. The DECLARE CURSOR statement must appear in your program before any statement operating on the cursor. Depending on the SQL implementation, this statement can be placed in either the WORKING-STORAGE SECTION or the PROCEDURE DIVISION of your COBOL program. The DECLARE CURSOR statement has the following form:

```
EXEC SQL
    DECLARE cursor-name CURSOR FOR
        SELECT statement
END-EXEC.
```

COMMAND DISCUSSION

1. The cursor name is the name assigned to the cursor structure.

2. The SELECT statement defines the query and indicates the rows to be retrieved.

3. The DECLARE CURSOR statement is declarative; the query is not executed at this time. Hence, no records are made available to the COBOL program when the DECLARE CURSOR statement is executed.

4. The rows retrieved by the query can be visualized as a table, technically referred to as the "active set of the cursor."

For example, to establish a cursor structure to retrieve the names and grade point averages of all students in a specific major, the following structure is declared:

Host variable is defined in the WORKING-STORAGE SECTION to allow the user to enter the desired major.

```
DECLARE STUDENTMAJOR CURSOR FOR
    SELECT  SNAME, GPA
    FROM    STUDENT
    WHERE   MAJOR = ':HMAJOR'
```

Note that there is no INTO clause when SELECT is used in the DECLARE CURSOR statement.

STUDENTMAJOR is the name of the cursor structure for all students in a given major.

Along with the cursor structure is a pointer, called a **cursor,** that indicates the current position within the structure. Once the cursor structure is declared, the cursor can be manipulated in the PROCEDURE DIVISION using the following statements:

```
OPEN
FETCH
CLOSE
```

Opening the Cursor

The DECLARE CURSOR statement in the WORKING-STORAGE SECTION of your COBOL program defines the structure of the cursor but does not retrieve any data. When the cursor structure is opened, the SELECT statement defined in the DECLARE CURSOR statement is executed and the set of records is stored in the cursor structure. The OPEN statement looks like this:

```
EXEC SQL
    OPEN   cursor-name
END-EXEC.
```

COMMAND DISCUSSION

1. The query associated with the cursor name in the OPEN statement is executed, and the "active set" of rows is retrieved.

2. The current value of any host variable in the WHERE clause of the SELECT statement is used to determine which rows make up the current active set.

3. The cursor is positioned just before the first row in the active set.

4. The cursor structure must be opened before any data can be retrieved from it.

For example, the statement

OPEN   STUDENTMAJOR

in the PROCEDURE DIVISION results in the following cursor structure:

CURSOR Structure When First Opened

STUDENTMAJOR

SNAME	GPA
POIRIER	3.2
FAGIN	2.2
MEGLIN	2.8
QUICK	3.5

Cursor position. ——————

Active set. ——

Fetching Records and Testing SQLCODE

Once you have opened the cursor structure, you can use the FETCH statement to retrieve the next row from the set of data in the cursor structure and to place values from that row into host variables. The form of this statement is

```
EXEC SQL
    FETCH   cursor-name
    INTO      host-variable1 [, host-variable2] ...
END-EXEC.
```

COMMAND DISCUSSION

1. Executing the FETCH statement advances the position of the cursor to the next row in the set of data in the named cursor. The first time FETCH is executed, the cursor is moved to the first row of the cursor structure.

2. The data values in the row to which the cursor is currently pointing are moved to the host variables contained in the INTO clause. Once the data values are in the host variables, your program can process them.

For example, Figure 10.4 illustrates a COBOL segment to retrieve one row at a time from the STUDENTMAJOR cursor structure.

FIGURE 10.4   COBOL Segment with Cursor Structure

```
WORKING-STORAGE SECTION.
      EXEC SQL
           DECLARE  STUDENTMAJOR  CURSOR FOR
                SELECT  SNAME, GPA
                FROM    STUDENT
                WHERE   MAJOR = :HMAJOR
      END-EXEC.

PROCEDURE DIVISION.

A000-MAIN.
      PERFORM B010-MAJOR-CHOICE.
      PERFORM B020-OPEN-CURSOR-STR.
      PERFORM B030-FETCH-RECD.
      PERFORM B040-PROCESS UNTIL SQLCODE = 100.
      STOP RUN.

B010-MAJOR-CHOICE.
      ...

B020-OPEN-CURSOR-STR.
      EXEC SQL
           OPEN  STUDENTMAJOR
      END-EXEC.

B030-FETCH-RECD.
      EXEC SQL
           FETCH  STUDENTMAJOR
           INTO   :HSNAME, :HGPA
      END-EXEC.

B040-PROCESS.
      DISPLAY   HSNAME, ' ', HGPA.
      PERFORM   B030-FETCH-RECD.
```

As a result of the execution of these statements, the DATA DIVISION can be conceptualized as follows after the first execution of the FETCH statement:

WORKING-STORAGE SECTION of COBOL Program
after Execution of First FETCH Statement

Host variables.

HSNAME	HGPA
POIRIER	3.2

Result of FETCH statement.

Comunication area.

SQLCODE
0

Cursor Structure

STUDENTMAJOR

Cursor position.

SNAME	GPA
POIRIER	3.2
FAGIN	2.2
MEGLIN	2.8
QUICK	3.5

Active set.

Normally, FETCH is executed repeatedly, in a loop structure, until end-of-data is reached. When there are no more rows in the active set, the "not found" (end-of-data) condition, SQLCODE = 100, is returned to the SQL communication area. When this condition occurs, no record is retrieved. Instead, control of the program is transferred to some other part of the program, such as a module that prints summary results or closes the cursor structure.

Closing the Cursor

The CLOSE statement removes the pointer from the cursor structure. The active set of records is no longer defined, and no rows can be fetched until the cursor structure is opened again. The form of this statement is

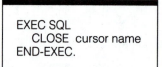

```
EXEC SQL
    CLOSE  cursor name
END-EXEC.
```

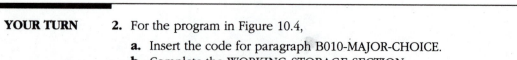

YOUR TURN   **2.** For the program in Figure 10.4,

    a. Insert the code for paragraph B010-MAJOR-CHOICE.

    b. Complete the WORKING-STORAGE SECTION.

A Complete Program

Figure 10.5 illustrates a complete COBOL program that retrieves a list of courses in which a student is currently enrolled. Since most full-time students are enrolled in more than one course, the program uses a cursor structure.

FIGURE 10.5   COBOL Program Displaying a Student's Course Schedule

```
          IDENTIFICATION DIVISION.
          PROGRAM-ID. COURSES.

          ENVIRONMENT DIVISION.

          DATA DIVISION.
          WORKING-STORAGE SECTION.

1         EXEC SQL  BEGIN DECLARE SECTION END-EXEC.

          01  HSID      PIC  XXX.
          01  HSNAME    PIC  X(15).
          01  HCRSNBR   PIC  X(6).
          01  HCNAME    PIC  X(10).

          EXEC SQL  END DECLARE SECTION    END-EXEC.

2         EXEC SQL
              DECLARE STUDENT TABLE
                  ( SID       CHAR(3)  NOT NULL,
                    SNAME     CHAR(10),
                    SEX       CHAR(1),
                    MAJOR     CHAR(3),
                    GPA       DECIMAL(3,2) )
          END-EXEC.

2         EXEC SQL
              DECLARE CRSENRL TABLE
                  ( SID       CHAR(3)  NOT NULL,
                    CRSNBR    CHAR(6)  NOT NULL,
                    GRADE     CHAR(1) )
          END-EXEC.

2         EXEC SQL
              DECLARE COURSE TABLE
                  ( CRSNBR    CHAR(6)  NOT NULL,
                    CNAME     CHAR(15),
                    DEPT      CHAR(3),
                    RANK      CHAR(4),
                    SALARY    INTEGER )
          END-EXEC.

3         EXEC SQL
              INCLUDE SQLCA
          END-EXEC.
```

Establishes the host variables used in SQL statements.

(continued on next page)

4
```
     EXEC SQL
         DECLARE STUDENTCOURSE CURSOR FOR ──────── Defines cursor
         SELECT    SNAME, CRSNBR, CNAME                    structure.
         FROM      STUDENT, COURSE, CRSENRL
         WHERE     SID = :HSID
           AND     STUDENT.SID = CRSENRL.SID
           AND     CRSENRL.CRSNBR = COURSE.CRSNBR
     END-EXEC.

 PROCEDURE DIVISION.

 A000-MAIN.
     PERFORM B010-GETID.
     PERFORM B020-OPEN.
     PERFORM B030-PROCESS.
     PERFORM B040-CLOSE.
     STOP RUN.

 B010-GETID.
     DISPLAY ' ENTER STUDENT ID: '.
     ACCEPT HSID.

 B020-OPEN.
```
5
```
     EXEC SQL
         OPEN STUDENTCOURSE ──────────── Cursor structure now
     END-EXEC.                               contains the records
                                             of the query.
 B030-PROCESS.
     PERFORM C010-RD-STU-COURSE.
```
6
```
     IF SQLCODE = 0
         PERFORM C020-DISPLAY-NAME
         PERFORM C030-COLUMN-HEADING
```
7
```
         PERFORM C040-COURSE-DETAIL UNTIL SQLCODE = 100
         PERFORM C050-END-OUTPUT
     ELSE IF SQLCODE = 100
         PERFORM C060-ERROR
     ELSE IF SQLCODE < 0
         PERFORM C070-ERROR.
```
8
```
 B040-CLOSE.
     EXEC SQL
         CLOSE STUDENTCOURSE
     END-EXEC.

 C010-RD-STU-COURSE.                     Transfers current row
```
9
```
     EXEC SQL                            of the cursor structure
         FETCH   STUDENTCOURSE ──────────── to host variables.
         INTO    :HSNAME, :HCRSNBR, :HCNAME
     END-EXEC.

 C020-DISPLAY-NAME.
     DISPLAY ' NAME     :  ', HSNAME
     DISPLAY '   '.

 C030-COLUMN-HEADING.
     DISPLAY ' COURSE         COURSE NAME'.
     DISPLAY ' NUMBER '.
```

(continued on next page)

```
C040-COURSE-DETAIL.
    DISPLAY HCRSNBR, '      ', HCNAME.
    PERFORM C010-RD-STU-COURSE. ——————— Gets next record from
                                         the cursor structure.
C050-END-OUTPUT.
    DISPLAY ' '.
    DISPLAY ' *** End Of Output *** .

C060-ERROR.
    DISPLAY ' No Data Found for Student with This ID'.

C070-ERROR.
    DISPLAY ' ERROR — CODE # IS : ', SQLCODE.
```

Sample output:

```
ENTER STUDENT ID: 218

NAME   :   RICHARDS

COURSE    COURSE NAME
NUMBER

ACC610    BASIC ACCOUNTING
ACC661    TAXATION
MGT630    INTRO TO MANAGEMENT

*** End of Output ***
```

The following points refer to sections in the program that are numbered on the left:

1. The host variables are defined.

2. The tables used in the program are declared.

3. The communication area is declared.

4. The cursor structure is defined. At this point, no rows have been selected.

5. The SELECT statement within the DECLARE CURSOR statement is processed. The set of records representing the courses in which a specific student is enrolled is now made available to the program.

6. The result of the FETCH statement is tested to determine if it worked correctly. If the FETCH statement worked correctly (SQLCODE = 0), then the student's name and column headings are displayed. If SQLCODE didn't work correctly, then it is tested to determine if there is no data in the cursor structure or if a serious error has occurred.

7. The STUDENTCOURSE cursor structure is repeatedly read and displayed until end-of-data (SQLCODE = 100) occurs.

8. The cursor structure is closed. The records can no longer be fetched.

9. The FETCH statement is executed repeatedly to read the next record from the cursor structure into the host variables HSNAME, HCRSNBR, and HCNAME.

YOUR TURN

3. In the program in Figure 10.5, what would happen if the first two statements in paragraph A000-MAIN were switched? The code would look like

```
A000-MAIN.
    PERFORM B020-OPEN.
    PERFORM B010-GETID.
    ...
```

KEEPING THE DATABASE CURRENT: WITHOUT CURSORS

File maintenance performed via interactive SQL is tedious and should be used only when there are a small number of changes that need attention or when the updating is simple.

A more common approach is to embed the SQL file maintenance commands (INSERT, UPDATE, and DELETE) directly in a host program. This approach to updating has several advantages:

- The data entry process is easier to follow since instructions can be provided, formatted screens can be designed, etc.

- The data can be checked to ensure the integrity of the database.

- The consistency of data for a sequence of SQL statements can be ensured.

INSERT Command

Just as in interactive SQL, the INSERT command is used to add rows to a table. However, the embedded version can be generalized through the inclusion of host variables in the VALUES clause instead of constant values.

Figure 10.6 illustrates a COBOL program that adds a student to the STUDENT table.

FIGURE 10.6   COBOL Program: Inserting a Row

```
        PROCEDURE DIVISION.

        A000-MAIN.
            PERFORM B010-DATAENTRY.
1           PERFORM B020-INSERT UNTIL HSID = ' '.
            STOP RUN.
```

(continued on next page)

```
2          B010-DATAENTRY.
              DISPLAY 'Student ID        : ' WITH NO ADVANCING.
              ACCEPT HSID.
              DISPLAY 'Student Name   : ' WITH NO ADVANCING.
              ACCEPT  HSNAME.
              DISPLAY 'Sex              : ' WITH NO ADVANCING.
              ACCEPT HSEX.
              DISPLAY 'Major            : ' WITH NO ADVANCING.
              ACCEPT HMAJOR.

3          B020-INSERT.
              EXEC SQL
                 INSERT INTO STUDENT(SID,SNAME,SEX,MAJOR)
                 VALUES(:HSID, :HSNAME, :HSEX, :HMAJOR)
              END-EXEC.

              DISPLAY ' '.
              DISPLAY '*** 1 RECORD ADDED ***'.

              PERFORM B010-DATAENTRY.
```

Sample output:

```
Student ID    :  193
Student Name  :  Miller
Sex           :  F
Major         :  FIN

*** 1 RECORD ADDED ***
```

The following comments refer to sections in the program that are numbered on the left:

1. The program stores data on a student one row at a time until the user terminates the program by entering a blank for student ID.

2. The data to be added to the STUDENT table are entered into the host variables during the execution of paragraph B010-DATAENTRY.

3. The values stored in the host variables are stored in one row of the STUDENT table.

UPDATE Command

The UPDATE command can be used in a COBOL program to change the values of one or more columns in one or more rows of a given table. The format of the UPDATE command is the same as that used in interactive SQL.

Let's look at a COBOL segment that changes a single row in a table. In the following sample program, a row in the STUDENT table is updated to reflect a change in a student's major.

```
PROCEDURE DIVISION.

A000-MAIN.
    PERFORM B010-DATAENTRY.
    PERFORM B020-UPDATE.
    STOP RUN.

B010-DATAENTRY.
    DISPLAY 'Student ID   : '.
    ACCEPT HSID.
    DISPLAY 'New Major   : '.
    ACCEPT NEWMAJOR.

B020-UPDATE.
    EXEC SQL
       UPDATE STUDENT
          SET    MAJOR  = :NEWMAJOR
          WHERE  SID  = :HSID
    END-EXEC.
```

Sample output:

```
Student ID  : 218
New Major  : FIN
```

A second sample program illustrates changes to multiple rows in a table. In this example, the Accounting faculty members receive a 10 percent salary increase.

```
PROCEDURE DIVISION.

A000-MAIN.
    PERFORM B010-DATAENTRY.
    PERFORM B020-UPDATE.
    STOP RUN.

B010-DATAENTRY.
    DISPLAY 'Department: '.
    ACCEPT HDEPT.
    DISPLAY 'Percent Increase: '.
    ACCEPT INCREASE.

B020-UPDATE.
    EXEC SQL
       UPDATE FACULTY
          SET    SALARY = SALARY * (1 + :INCREASE/100)
          WHERE  DEPT = :HDEPT
    END-EXEC.
```

Sample output:

```
Department:      ACC
Percent Increase: 10
```

DELETE Command

The DELETE command removes one or more rows from a given table. The format of the command is the same as that used in interactive SQL.

The following COBOL program illustrates deleting a single row from a table. In this example, a student course record is deleted when a student drops a course.

```
PROCEDURE DIVISION.

A000-MAIN.
     PERFORM B010-DATAENTRY.
     PERFORM B020-DELETE.
     STOP RUN.

B010-DATAENTRY.
     DISPLAY 'Student ID        : '.
     ACCEPT HSID.
     DISPLAY 'Course Number : '.
     ACCEPT HCRSNBR.

B020-DELETE.
     EXEC SQL
        DELETE FROM CRSENRL
        WHERE  SID = :HSID
           AND  CRSNBR = :HCRSNBR
     END-EXEC.
```

Sample output:

```
Student ID       : 763
Course Number : FIN602
```

The next program illustrates deleting multiple rows from a table. In this example, all rows in the CRSENRL table are deleted so that the student course records for the new term can be inserted.

```
PROCEDURE DIVISION.

A000-MAIN.
     PERFORM B010-DELETE.
     STOP RUN.

B010-DELETE.
     EXEC SQL
        DELETE FROM CRSENRL
     END-EXEC.
```

Note that both DELETE and UPDATE statements can affect multiple rows without using a cursor structure.

KEEPING THE DATABASE CURRENT: WITH CURSORS

When reading and updating many records, an approach using a cursor structure is appropriate. When a row from a cursor structure is fetched, the values of columns can be displayed, and appropriate changes or deletions can be made to the record. For example, the updating of the CRSENRL table to reflect the grades received by students in a course would be an appropriate use of this approach.

Before we review a sample program that updates data in a table, there are some changes to the DECLARE CURSOR and UPDATE statements that need to be examined.

DECLARE CURSOR Command

An additional clause, FOR UPDATE OF, must be included in the definition of the DECLARE CURSOR statement. This clause specifies all columns that can be updated. The form of this statement is

```
EXEC SQL
    DECLARE  cursor-name  CURSOR FOR
      SELECT statement
      [FOR UPDATE OF column-name1 [, column-name2] ...]
END-EXEC.
```

COMMAND DISCUSSION

The columns that can be updated are indicated following the FOR UPDATE OF clause.

UPDATE Command

To update the current row of the cursor structure, use the WHERE CURRENT OF clause of the UPDATE statement. This version of the UPDATE statement is called the **positioned UPDATE.** The general form of this statement is

```
EXEC SQL
    UPDATE   table-name
      SET    column-name1 = expression1
             [, column-name2 = expression2] ...
      [WHERE CURRENT OF  cursor-name ]
END-EXEC.
```

COMMAND DISCUSSION

1. The cursor structure must be opened and positioned (using FETCH) on a row before the UPDATE command can be executed.

2. Each execution of the UPDATE statement updates one row—the row at which the cursor is positioned.

3. The only columns that can be updated are those listed in the FOR UPDATE OF clause of the DECLARE CURSOR statement.

4. The cursor is not moved by the execution of the UPDATE statement. The FETCH statement moves the cursor.

Now you're ready to examine a COBOL program that updates a table using a cursor structure. Figure 10.7 illustrates a COBOL program that accepts grades entered by a clerk and updates the CRSENRL table for each student in a specified course.

FIGURE 10.7 COBOL Program: Updating a Table Using a Cursor Structure

```
        WORKING-STORAGE SECTION.
            ...

1       EXEC SQL
            DECLARE STU_CLASS_ROSTER CURSOR FOR
                SELECT  SID, GRADE
                FROM    CRSENRL
                WHERE   CRSNBR = :HCRSNBR
                FOR UPDATE OF GRADE
        END-EXEC.

        PROCEDURE DIVISION.

        A000-MAIN.
            PERFORM B010-GET-COURSE.
            PERFORM B020-OPEN.
2           PERFORM B030-FETCH.
            PERFORM B040-UPDATE-PROCESS  UNTIL SQLCODE = 100.
            PERFORM B050-CLOSE.
            STOP RUN.

        B010-GET-COURSE.
            DISPLAY 'Course Number: '.
            ACCEPT HCRSNBR.

        B020-OPEN.
            EXEC SQL
                OPEN STU_CLASS_ROSTER
            END-EXEC.
```

(continued on next page)

```
            B030-FETCH.
                EXEC SQL
                    FETCH STU_CLASS_ROSTER
                    INTO   :HSID, HGRADE
                END-EXEC.

            B040-UPDATE-PROCESS.
                PERFORM C010-DATAENTRY.
                PERFORM C020-UPDATE.
                PERFORM B030-FETCH.

            B050-CLOSE.
                EXEC SQL
                    CLOSE STU_CLASS_ROSTER
                END-EXEC.

  3         C010-DATAENTRY.
                DISPLAY 'Student ID : ', HSID.
                DISPLAY ' '.
                DISPLAY 'Grade      :'.
                ACCEPT  HGRADE. ———————————————— Clerk enters grade.

  4         C020-UPDATE.
                EXEC SQL
                    UPDATE CRSENRL
                        SET   GRADE = :HGRADE
                        WHERE CURRENT OF STU_CLASS_ROSTER
                END-EXEC.
```

The following comments relate to sections in the program that are numbered on the left:

1. The active set represents all the student course records for a specified course.
2. The first student course record is fetched.
3. The clerk enters the grade for the indicated student.
4. The current record in the cursor structure is updated using the grade entered in paragraph C010-DATAENTRY.

DELETE Command

To delete a row using the cursor structure approach requires the use of the DECLARE CURSOR statement and the "positioned" DELETE statement. The positioned DELETE statement has the following form:

```
EXEC SQL
    DELETE table-name
        WHERE CURRENT OF cursor-name
END-EXEC.
```

COMMAND DISCUSSION

1. The current position of the cursor determines the row to be deleted.

2. After the deletion occurs, the cursor goes into a "between" state: the cursor is open but has no current row until you reposition it by using a FETCH statement.

Note: The FOR UPDATE clause is not used in defining the DECLARE CURSOR statement when you are deleting records. The same format used for selection is used for deletion.

YOUR TURN

4. For the program in Figure 10.7,

    a. Define the host variables that should be declared in the WORKING-STORAGE SECTION.

    b. Modify the DECLARE CURSOR statement so that you can display the student's name as well as the ID in C010-DATAENTRY.

This completes the section on keeping the database current. To conclude this chapter, we briefly discuss the process needed to execute an embedded SQL program using COBOL.

PREPARING THE COBOL PROGRAM FOR EXECUTION

Once your COBOL program is written, four steps must be performed before the program will run. (See Figure 10.8.)

Precompilation

A COBOL compiler does not recognize SQL statements. Therefore, before compiling a COBOL program with embedded SQL statements, the program is processed by a precompiler. The **precompiler** accepts your COBOL program as input and produces a modified source program that the COBOL compiler can process. The precompiler replaces each SQL statement with a COBOL CALL statement to the DBMS. The original SQL commands are included in the new source code as comments. In addition, the precompiler builds a file called the **database request module** (DBRM), which stores all the information on SQL statements used by the application program.

FIGURE 10.8   Steps Required to Run Embedded SQL

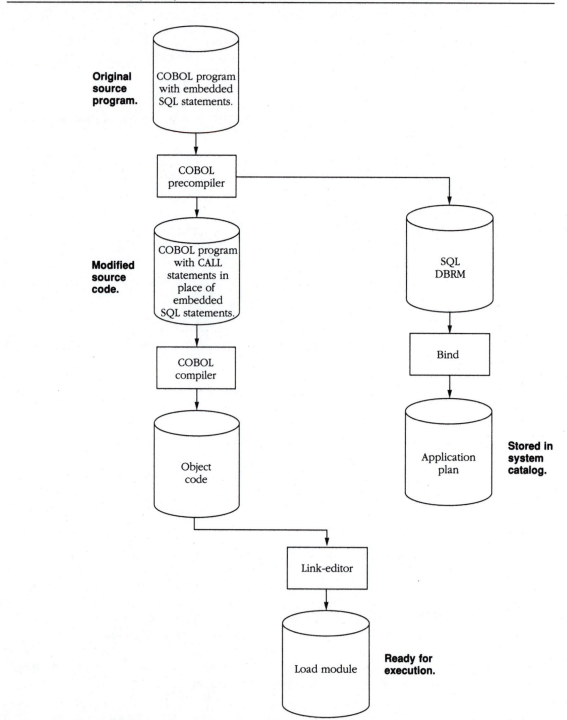

Compilation

After preprocessing is completed, the modified source code is input to the COBOL compiler. The COBOL object code is produced as a result of this step.

Bind

During the bind process, the following occurs:

- Checking precompiled SQL statements to verify that they are syntactically correct.

- Verifying that the issuer of the BIND command has been granted the appropriate privileges to execute the SQL operations specified in the DBRM.

- Choosing the most efficient access path to data.

Also during this step, the DBRM's SQL statements are converted to a set of procedures called an **application plan,** which is stored in the system catalog. The application plan identifies the processing that the DBMS must perform to each SQL statement when the program is executed.

Link-Edit

The object code is link-edited with other SQL routines to form a load module ready for execution. Now the program can be executed.

Video Rental, Inc. Case
CHAPTER ASSIGNMENT

1. **a.** Write a program to prepare the rental receipt.

   b. Incorporate into the program the insertion of the rental record (header and detail) and the update of the MOVIE table.

2. Write a program to update the tables when a rental return occurs.

Formatting Reports

Many users of SQL prefer more precise control over the appearance of their output than is possible when using the SELECT statement. For example, a user might want subtotals, different column headings, or a title on the actual report. The commands introduced in this appendix allow you to include these improvements in your output. Unfortunately, vendors of SQL products deviate in their implementation of this feature. Some vendors include a report formatting capability, while others do not have this capability. The material discussed in this appendix is based on ORACLE's version of SQL. If you are using a different implementation of SQL, check your reference manual to determine if and how report formats can be implemented.

Compare the two outputs in Figure A.1. The first version was developed using only the SELECT statement; the second version adds formatting commands to the SELECT statement that improve the output. Notice that Version B not only generates more information than Version A but it is also easier to read.

FIGURE A.1   Comparison between Formatted and Unformatted Output

VERSION A: Unformatted

```
SELECT      DEPT, FNAME, SALARY
FROM        FACULTY
ORDER BY    DEPT

DEPT    FNAME       SALARY

ACC     KENNEDY     30000
ACC     DARDEN      37000
FIN     JARDIN      33000
FIN     PETERS      45000
MGT     BARGES      35000
MGT     WARD        20000
MGT     PIERCE      22000
MKT     SAMPLE      25000
```

(continued on next page)

VERSION B: Formatted

```
TTITLE 'S A L A R Y   R E P O R T'
COLUMN SALARY      FORMAT $999,999.
BREAK ON DEPT      SKIP 1
COMPUTE SUM OF   SALARY ON DEPT

SELECT     DEPT, FNAME, SALARY
FROM       FACULTY
ORDER BY   DEPT
```

**Formatting
commands.**

Wed Apr 22   page 1

S A L A R Y   R E P O R T

DEPT	FNAME	SALARY
ACC	KENNEDY	$30,000.
	DARDEN	$37,000.
***		
		$67,000.
FIN	JARDIN	$33,000.
	PETERS	$45,000.
***		
		$78,000.
MGT	BARGES.	$35,000.
	WARD	$20,000.
	PIERCE	$22,000.
***		
		$77,000.
MKT	SAMPLE	$25,000.
***		
		$25,000.

By adding formatting commands to the SELECT statement, you can

- change the column headings.
- put titles at the top or bottom of a page.
- break reports into groups of rows.
- compute subtotals and totals for groups of rows.
- round numbers to a specified number of decimal places.
- insert commas and dollar signs into numbers.

ORACLE'S version of SQL supports five formatting commands that enable a user to produce formatted output that improves the appearance of reports. These commands include

COLUMN	Changes column heading and formats values within a column.
BREAK	Places blank lines between groups of rows.
COMPUTE	Computes subtotals and totals for groups of rows.
TTITLE	Places a title at the top of a page.
BTITLE	Places a title at the bottom of a page.

COLUMN COMMANDS

The COLUMN command allows you to change the column heading automatically displayed with the SELECT statement to another heading. In its simplest form, the command has the following syntax:

```
COLUMN column-name  HEADING 'character string'
```

COMMAND DISCUSSION

1. COLUMN is the keyword that indicates you are changing a column heading from the heading automatically provided by SQL when using the SELECT statement. The column for which the heading is being changed follows the keyword COLUMN.

2. The string that follows the keyword HEADING is the new column heading to be displayed with the output.

3. COLUMN operates on only one column at a time. If two or more headings are to be changed, a separate COLUMN command is executed for each column.

EXAMPLE A.1   Suppose you want to change the format of reported data in Example 3.1. In that example, the SQL statement

```
SELECT  SNAME
FROM    STUDENT
```

results in

```
SNAME

POIRIER
PARKER
RICHARDS
PELNICK
FAGIN
MEGLIN
LEE
GAMBRELL
QUICK
ANDERSON
```

(continued on next page)

You may want to change the column heading SNAME to a more descriptive heading such as STUDENT NAME. To do so, you key

```
COLUMN  SNAME  HEADING 'STUDENT NAME'
SELECT   SNAME
FROM     STUDENT
```

which results in

New column heading. ——— STUDENT NAME

```
POIRIER
PARKER
RICHARDS
FAGIN
MEGLIN
LEE
GAMBRELL
QUICK
ANDERSON
```

Column headings can appear on more than one line by placing the bar (I) character between the words that you want on separate lines. For example, if you want the words STUDENT and NAME to appear on separate lines, you key the COLUMN command

```
COLUMN  SNAME  HEADING 'STUDENT I NAME'
```

which results in

A two-line heading. ——— STUDENT
NAME

```
POIRIER
PARKER
RICHARDS
PELNICK
FAGIN
MEGLIN
LEE
GAMBRELL
QUICK
ANDERSON
```

YOUR TURN

1. Write the COLUMN commands necessary to obtain the following headings:

   a. COURSE NUMBER   COURSE TITLE

   b. STUDENT   GRADE
       NAME   POINT
                         MAJOR   AVERAGE

The COLUMN command can also be used to format column data. Thus, the values within a column can appear with dollar signs, commas can be added to numbers, and output values can be reported to a desired number of decimal positions.

In this form, the COLUMN command has the following syntax:

```
COLUMN expression   FORMAT format-mask
              or
       column-name
```

The items in Table A.1 identify a subset of format symbols that are used in ORACLE's version of SQL.

TABLE A.1   Selected Format-masks

Format Symbol	Description	Value Stored	Format-mask	Output Displayed
9	Each nine (9) represents a digit within a numeric column.	25.876 25.876	999 9999	25 25
.	The decimal point (.) represents the position where a decimal point is to be inserted into a value.	25 25.876 25.876 25.876	99. 99.9 99.99 99.9999	25. 25.9 25.88 25.8760
,	The comma (,) indicates a comma is to be printed between every third digit to the left of the decimal point.	6082.69	99,999.9	6,082.7
$	The dollar sign ($) indicates the position where a dollar sign is to be printed.	6082.69	$9,999.	$6,082.

EXAMPLE A.2   To format the average faculty salary report from Example 4.7, key the following:

(continued on next page)

```
COLUMN AVG(SALARY) FORMAT $99,999.99

SELECT    DEPT, AVG(SALARY)
FROM      FACULTY
GROUP BY  DEPT
HAVING    AVG(SALARY) > 25000
```

which results in

```
DEPT      AVG(SALARY)

ACC       $33,500.00
FIN       $39,000.00
MGT       $25,666.67
```

The COLUMN command can be used to combine heading and format information. In this form, the command has the following syntax:

```
COLUMN column-name  HEADING 'character string' FORMAT format-mask
              or
          expression
```

Assume you want to modify the output of Eample 4.7 using the COLUMN command. Here is what the command would look like:

```
COLUMN AVG(SALARY) HEADING 'AVERAGE I SALARY'  FORMAT $99,999.

SELECT    DEPT, AVG(SALARY)
FROM      FACULTY
GROUP BY  DEPT
HAVING    AVG(SALARY) > 25000
```

which results in

```
DEPT      AVERAGE ─────────────────────── Improved heading.
          SALARY

ACC       $33,500.
FIN       $39,000.
MGT       $25,666.
```

BREAK COMMAND

Many reports that involve sorting can be made more readable by the use of the BREAK command. This command permits skipping lines between groups of records. For example, in a listing of faculty, skipping lines between the last faculty member in one department and the first faculty member in the next department can be done with this command. In addition, duplicate values in a column of a report can be suppressed. The format for the BREAK command is

```
BREAK ON  column-name  [SKIP n]
                       [PAGE]
```

COMMAND DISCUSSION

1. The column name following the keywords BREAK ON indicates the field in each row that is used to group records. This column name must also be specified in the ORDER BY clause of the SELECT statement; otherwise, the command will not work properly.

2. The SKIP keyword allows you to indicate the number of lines (n) to be skipped between groups. Instead of skipping lines, the PAGE keyword can be substituted. The PAGE keyword results in output for each group appearing on separate pages.

EXAMPLE A.3   A query to display the names of faculty members and their salaries ordered by department was entered using the following SELECT statement:

```
SELECT     DEPT, FNAME, SALARY
FROM       FACULTY
ORDER BY   DEPT
```

which resulted in

DEPT	FNAME	SALARY
ACC	KENNEDY	30000
ACC	DARDEN	37000
FIN	JARDIN	33000
FIN	PETERS	45000
MGT	BARGES	35000
MGT	WARD	20000
MGT	PIERCE	22000
MKT	SAMPLE	25000

(continued on next page)

To improve the format of the output by inserting a blank line between faculty in different departments, the following BREAK command is issued:

```
BREAK ON DEPT  SKIP 1
SELECT      DEPT, FNAME, SALARY
FROM        FACULTY
ORDER BY    DEPT
```

which results in

DEPT	FNAME	SALARY
ACC	KENNEDY	30000
	DARDEN	37000
FIN	JARDIN	33000
	PETERS	45000
MGT	BARGES	35000
	WARD	20000
	PIERCE	22000
MKT	SAMPLE	25000

Duplicate department codes are not printed.

Skips one line when group (DEPT) switches from ACC to FIN, from FIN to MGT, and so on.

COMPUTE COMMAND

Very often it is desirable to include group totals in reports. For example, the output of the previous example can be enhanced by including total salary paid in each department. Reports that include subtotals for groups of rows are often referred to as **control break** reports.

To obtain these control break reports, the COMPUTE command is used. This command has the following format:

```
COMPUTE SUM OF  sum-column  ON  break-column
```

COMMAND DISCUSSION

1. The sum column represents the column for which subtotals are accumulated.

2. The break column indicates the field in each row that is used to group records.

3. The COMPUTE command works in conjunction with the BREAK command. If the BREAK command is not entered, then subtotals cannot be computed.

EXAMPLE A.4   To obtain total departmental salaries along with individual faculty salaries, the following commands are needed:

```
BREAK ON DEPT  SKIP 1                          Note that both BREAK
COMPUTE SUM OF SALARY ON DEPT                   and COMPUTE are
                                               used.
SELECT      DEPT, FNAME, SALARY
FROM        FACULTY
ORDER BY    DEPT
```

which results in

DEPT	FNAME	SALARY	
ACC	KENNEDY	30000	
	DARDEN	37000	
***			
		67000	—— Group subtotal.
FIN	JARDIN	33000	
	PETERS	45000	
***			
		78000	
			—— Control break occurs
MGT	BARGES	35000	when department value
	WARD	20000	changes.
	PIERCE	22000	
***			
		77000	
MKT	SAMPLE	25000	
***			
		25000	

Duplicate department names are omitted.

REPORT TITLES

To include page titles in the output, the command TTITLE is used. This command places titles, page numbers, and the current date at the top of each page. The form of this command is

```
TTITLE 'page title '
```

Another command, BTITLE, places page titles at the bottom of each page. The form of this command is

```
BTITLE 'page title '
```

EXAMPLE A.5   To obtain the output shown in Figure A.1, Version B, the following commands are used:

```
TTITLE 'S A L A R Y   R E P O R T'
COLUMN  SALARY  FORMAT $999,999.
BREAK ON  DEPT  SKIP 1
COMPUTE SUM OF  SALARY  ON DEPT

SELECT       DEPT, FNAME, SALARY
FROM         FACULTY
ORDER BY   DEPT
```

The final enhancements to the report appear as follows:

Wed Apr 22   page 1

S A L A R Y   R E P O R T

DEPT	FNAME	SALARY
ACC	KENNEDY	$30,000.
	DARDEN	$37,000.
***		
		$67,000.
FIN	JARDIN	$33,000.
	PETERS	$45,000.
***		
		$78,000.
MGT	BARGES	$35,000.
	WARD	$20,000.
	PIERCE	$22,000.
***		
		$77,000.
MKT	SAMPLE	$25,000.
***		
		$25,000.

$67,000. ——————— **Group subtotal.**

Control break occurs when department value changes.

Appendix B *Storing, Retrieving, and Generalizing Queries*

When you enter an SQL statement, it is stored in a temporary storage area. If you enter a new statement or log off the computer system, the statement currently in the temporary storage area is no longer available. Fortunately, complex queries that are used on a continuing basis can be stored permanently so they don't have to be reentered each time they have to be executed. Most implementations of SQL have the capability to store SQL commands; however, the specifics vary somewhat from implementation to implementation. In this appendix, we illustrate how ORACLE's implementation of SQL allows users to store queries.

A SAVE command is used to copy statements from the temporary storage area into permanent storage. The syntax of this command is

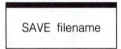

EXAMPLE B.1   A list of students is constantly being prepared. Store a query, which prepares a list of students, permanently in a file named STDNTLST.

The SQL statement

```
SELECT      SNAME, SEX, MAJOR, GPA
FROM        STUDENT
ORDER BY    MAJOR, SNAME
```

is entered into temporary storage. To store this statement permanently, the following command is issued:

SAVE STDNTLST   ┌─ **Name of file**
                                          │ **storing the**
         └────────────────────────────────┘ **SQL query.**

A message is displayed to let you know that the file has been stored.

Once STDNTLST is stored, it can be retrieved using the START command. The form of this command is

```
START filename
```

This command copies a file into the temporary storage area where the SQL statement is executed.

EXAMPLE B.2   Retrieve the student list query stored as STDNTLST.

The command

    START STDNTLST

retrieves the file STDNTLST, places it into temporary storage, and executes the query. The following results are displayed:

SNAME	SEX	MAJOR	GPA
RICHARDS	M	ACC	2.4
ANDERSON	M	ACC	3.7
PARKER	F	FIN	2.7
PELNICK	F	FIN	3.6
LEE	M	FIN	2.7
POIRIER	F	MGT	3.2
FAGIN	M	MGT	2.2
MEGLIN	M	MGT	2.8
QUICK	F	MGT	3.5
GAMBRELL	F	MKT	3.8

When you log off, the file STDNTLST is erased from the temporary storage area, but it still remains in permanent storage and can be retrieved again by following the same procedures.

A Dean of Students may need to list names and grade point averages of students in specific majors. Queries can be designed in such a manner that the user can enter specific values at the time of execution; this allows the Dean to list finance majors at one time and accounting majors at another. The use of a **substitution variable,** or placeholder, allows prompting for data at the time the SQL query is executed. The substitution variable consists of an ampersand (&) symbol followed by a number and is used in place of a constant or column name in the query. The system prompts the user for a value when the query is executed. The user responds to the prompt with a value, and then the query is executed.

EXAMPLE B.3   The Dean of Students wants to retrieve data on students in a particular major; however, the specific major varies, depending on the situation.

The SQL statement

```
SELECT   SNAME, GPA
FROM     STUDENT
WHERE    MAJOR = '&1'
```

Quotes surround the substitution variable because the value input is a character string. If the value were numeric, quotes would not be needed.

results in

Enter Value for 1: ACC

The user enters the major following the prompt.

After the user responds, the following output, listing accounting majors, is displayed:

SNAME	GPA	
RICHARDS	2.4	**These students are**
ANDERSON	3.7	**accounting majors.**

Upon execution of the SELECT statement, the substitution variable within the query is detected, which results in a prompt being displayed. The user responds to the prompt by entering ACC, and the names of students majoring in accounting, along with their grade point averages, are displayed.

The SELECT statement can be stored permanently by issuing the command

```
SAVE  MAJORLST
```

To execute this query at a later date, the user retrieves the stored file by issuing the command

```
START  MAJORLST
```

The query is executed, the user is prompted for a specific value, and the students for the specified major are displayed.

For example, at a later date, the Dean wants a list of finance majors.

The Dean enters the command

```
START  MAJORLST
```

and the following prompt appears:

Enter Value for 1: FIN

(continued on next page)

After the user responds to the prompt, the following output, listing finance majors, is displayed:

SNAME	GPA
PARKER	2.7
PELNICK	3.6
LEE	2.7

Background for Video Rental, Inc.

The owner of Video Rental, Inc. has just installed a computer system to keep track of movie club members, movie inventory, and rental and return transactions. Before we begin, let's describe each of these components.

Members A customer must be a member of Video Rental in order to rent movies from the company. A new member completes an application and elects to become either an annual member ($15 per year) or a lifetime member ($50 one-time charge). The member supplies information such as name, address, and phone number. When the application is approved, the member is assigned an identification number and issued a membership card. Additionally, the data on the member is added to the computer file.

Movie Inventory Currently, the store has 350 movies available for rent. (For simplicity, we'll assume no duplicate copies of movies are maintained in inventory.) When a new movie is received, it is added to the movie inventory file. The following data is maintained for each movie: movie ID number, movie title, purchase date, purchase cost, movie rating, movie category (comedy, action, drama, childrens, etc.), and status (in store/available for rent, rented, damaged, etc.).

Rental Transaction Rental transactions are recorded using a microcomputer at the rental desk. When a member rents a movie, the clerk enters the member's ID, the date rented, the date due, and the movie ID.

The member pays the rental charge in advance; each movie rents for $2 per day. The computer prints a rental receipt that is given to the member.

Rental Return Transaction When a member returns a movie, the rental record is updated to reflect the date returned. In addition, the movie inventory record is updated to indicate the movie is in the store and available for rent.

The database for this case consists of four tables, as follows:

a. MEMBER Table   All active members are stored in this table, one row for each member.

b. MOVIE Table   All movies owned by Video Rental are stored in this table, one row per movie.

c. RENTHEAD Table   Each rental transaction (receipt) is a row in this table.

d. RENTDETL Table   For each transaction (receipt), there is a separate row for each movie rented.

Figure C.1 describes the layout of each table. Sample data for use with the Video Rental tables appears in Figure C.2.

FIGURE C.1   Layout of Tables for Video Rental, Inc.

a. MEMBER Table

Column Description	Column Name	Data Type	Length	Decimal Places	Nulls Allowed	Codes
Member ID number	MEMID	Character	3		No	
Member name	MEMNAME	Character	10		No	
Member address	ADDRESS	Character	15		Yes	
City and state	CTYST	Character	15		Yes	
Date of membership	MEMDATE	Date			Yes	MM/DD/YYYY
Type of membership	MEMTYPE	Character	1		Yes	A=Annual L=Life

b. MOVIE Table

Column Description	Column Name	Data Type	Length	Decimal Places	Nulls Allowed	Codes
Movie ID number	MOVID	Character	4		No	
Movie title	TITLE	Character	35		No	
Movie category	CAT	Character	2		Yes	COmedy ACtion CHildrens HOrror
Movie rating	RATING	Character	4		Yes	G, PG, PG13, R, X
Date movie purchased	PURDATE	Date			Yes	MM/DD/YYYY
Cost of movie	PURCOST	Decimal	5	2	Yes	
Status of movie	STATUS	Character	1		Yes	R=Rented I=In Store D=Damaged

c. RENTHEAD Table

Column Description	Column Name	Data Type	Length	Decimal Places	Nulls Allowed	Codes
Invoice number	INVNBR	Integer			No	
Member ID number	MEMID	Character	3		No	
Date rented	RENTDATE	Date			No	MM/DD/YYYY
Date due	DUEDATE	Date			No	MM/DD/YYYY
Date returned	RETRNDTE	Date			Yes	MM/DD/YYYY

(continued on next page)

d. RENTDETL Table

Column Description	Column Name	Data Type	Length	Decimal Places	Nulls Allowed	Codes
Invoice number	INVNBR	Integer			No	
Movie ID number	MOVID	Character	4		No	
Total rental charge for this movie	CHARGE	Decimal	6	2	No	

FIGURE C.2   Sample Data for Video Rental, Inc. Tables

a. MEMBER Table

MEMID	MEMNAME	ADDRESS	CTYST	MEMDATE	MEMTYPE
101	ALLRED	105 FITTS COURT	PEACEDALE, RI	2/8/87	A
105	MCLEAVEY	97 KINGS ROAD	NARRAGANSETT, RI	2/24/87	L
107	MOJENA	1 NORTH ST	WAKEFIELD, RI	2/28/87	A
109	KIM	116 CRANK ROAD	KINGSTON, RI	3/3/87	A
113	DELLA	3 FLOWER ST	WAKEFIELD, RI	3/3/87	L
115	SASSY	10 GREY WOODS	PEACEDALE, RI	3/7/87	A
119	BUDNICK	19 ALCO LANE	WAKEFIELD, RI	3/10/87	A
123	WESTIN	97 SIMPLE RD	WAKEFIELD, RI	3/12/87	L

b. MOVIE Table

MOVID	TITLE	CAT	RATING	PURDATE	PURCOST	STATUS
1001	Back to the Future	CO	PG	02/10/87	22	R
1002	Flight of the Navigator	CH	PG	02/14/87	18	R
1003	Cobra	AC	PG13	02/18/87	23	I
1004	Friday the 13th: Part VI	HO	R	02/18/87	23	I
1005	Down and Out in Beverly Hills	CO	PG	02/20/87	22	I
1006	My Little Pony	CH	G	02/20/87	19	I
1007	Firewalker	AC	PG13	02/20/87	23	I
1008	Nightmare on Elm Street 2	HO	R	02/22/87	25	I
1009	Ferris Bueller's Day Off	CO	G	03/01/87	22	I
1010	Pinocchio	CH	G	03/03/87	18	I
1011	Heartbreak Ridge	AC	PG13	03/07/87	23	I
1012	Poltergeist II	HO	R	03/07/87	25	R
1013	Ruthless People	CO	PG13	03/12/87	20	R
1014	Sleeping Beauty	CH	G	03/14/87	24	I
1015	Indiana Jones and the Temple of Doom	AC	PG	03/17/87	22	R
1016	The Fly	HO	PG13	03/24/87	19	I
1017	The Boy Who Could Fly	CH	PG	03/29/87	22	I
1018	Top Gun	AC	PG13	04/02/87	25	I
1019	Transformers	CH	PG	04/04/87	20	I

(continued on next page)

c. RENTHEAD Table

INVNBR	MEMID	RENTDATE	DUEDATE	RETRNDTE
10557	105	5/2/87	5/3/87	5/3/87
10558	107	5/3/87	5/5/87	5/5/87
10559	119	5/6/87	5/7/87	5/7/87
10560	101	5/9/87	5/10/87	5/10/87
10561	115	5/11/87	5/12/87	
10562	105	5/11/87	5/13/87	
10563	107	5/11/87	5/12/87	

d. RENTDETL Table

INVNBR	MOVID	CHARGE
10557	1008	2
10558	1010	4
10558	1016	4
10558	1019	4
10559	1016	2
10559	1001	2
10560	1002	2
10560	1010	2
10561	1013	2
10562	1015	4
10562	1012	4
10563	1001	2
10563	1002	2

A Comparison of SQL Implementations

How to Use This Table: The left-hand side of the table lists the syntax of the more commonly used SQL commands. The first part of the table consists of commands that can be used in either interactive or embedded SQL. The second part of the table lists commands available only when developing embedded SQL programs. A vertical line in front of a command indicates a variation in syntax, between implementations, for the same command. Use the right-hand side of the table to determine if the command is available in the listed implementations of SQL.

The remaining portion of this appendix compares data types, operators, aggregate functions, arithmetic operators, table privileges, and rules for naming tables, views, and columns.

If you wish to look up more information on a specific command, use the text page reference column.

	DB2	SQL/DS	ORACLE	XDB	ANSI Standard	Text Page
COMMANDS FOR USE IN INTERACTIVE AND EMBEDDED SQL						
ALTER TABLE table-name ADD column-name data-type	x	x	x			101
ALTER TABLE table-name MODIFY column-name [new data-type]			x			

ALTER TABLE table-name
   {ADD column-name data-type}
   {DELETE column-name}
   {RENAME old-column-name new-column-name}
   {MODIFY old-column-name new-data-type}
				x		

CREATE [UNIQUE] INDEX index-name
ON table-name
   (column-name1 [DESC]
   [,column-name2 [DESC]] ...)
	x	x	x	x		104

CREATE TABLE table-name
   (column-name1 data-type [NOT NULL]
   [, column-name2 data-type [NOT NULL]] ...)
	x	x	x	x		13

	DB2	SQL/DS	ORACLE	XDB	ANSI Standard	Text Page

CREATE TABLE table-name
    (column-name1 data-type [NOT NULL] [UNIQUE]
    [, column-name2 data-type [NOT NULL] [UNIQUE]] ...)
					X	

CREATE VIEW view-name [(column-name1 [, column-name2]...)] AS SELECT-statement	X	X	X	X	X	84
DELETE FROM table-name [WHERE search-condition]	X	X	X	X	X	78
DROP INDEX index-name	X	X	X	X		109
DROP TABLE table-name	X	X	X	X		17
DROP VIEW view-name	X	X	X	X		90

GRANT {ALL}
        {privilege1 [,privilege2]...}
    ON   {table-name}
         {view-name}
    TO   {PUBLIC}
         {userid1 [,userid2]...}
    [WITH GRANT OPTION]
	X	X	X	X	X	93

INSERT INTO table-name [(column-name1 [, column-name2]...)] VALUES(value1 [, value2]...)	X	X	X	X	X	74
INSERT INTO table-name [(column-name1 [, column-name2]...)] SELECT-statement	X	X	X	X	X	76

REVOKE {ALL}
         {privilege1 [, privilege2] ...}
    ON   {table-name}
            {view-name}
    FROM {PUBLIC}
            {userid1 [, userid2] ...}
	X	X	X	X	X	97

SELECT [DISTINCT] {expression1 [, expression2]...}
                  {*}
    FROM   table-name1 [alias1] [, table-name2 [alias2]]...
    [WHERE   search-condition]
    [GROUP BY column-name1 [, column-name2]...
      [HAVING search-condition]]
    [ORDER BY column-name3 [DESC] [, column-name4 [DESC]] ...]
	X	X	X	X		18

† SELECT [DISTINCT] {expression1 [, expression2]...}
                  {*}
    FROM   table-name1 [alias1] [, table-name2 [alias2]]...
    [WHERE   search-condition]
    [GROUP BY column-name1 [, column-name2]...
      [HAVING search-condition]]
					X	

UPDATE table-name
    SET   column-name1 = expression1
            [, column-name2 = expression2] ...
    [WHERE search-condition]
	X	X	X	X	X	80

---

† Within interactive SQL, the ANSI Standard permits the result of a query to consist of only one row. Multiple-row SELECT operations are allowed within embedded SQL by using the DECLARE cursor statement.

	DB2	SQL/DS	ORACLE	XDB	ANSI Standard	Text Page
COMMANDS AVAILABLE FOR EMBEDDED SQL ONLY						
BEGIN DECLARE SECTION		X	X		X	113
CLOSE cursor-name	X	X	X		X	124

DECLARE cursor-name CURSOR FOR
    SELECT-statement
    [FOR UPDATE OF column-name1 [, column-name2] ...]
	X	X	X			120
						132

DECLARE cursor-name CURSOR FOR
    SELECT-statement
    [ORDER BY column-name1 [DESC] [, column-name2 [DESC]] ...]
					X	

DECLARE table-name TABLE	X					114
DELETE FROM table-name [WHERE CURRENT OF cursor-name]	X	X			X	131 134
END DECLARE SECTION	X		X		X	113
END-EXEC	X	X	X		X	111
EXEC SQL	X	X	X		X	111
FETCH cursor-name INTO :host-variable1 [, :host-variable2] ...	X	X	X		X	122
INCLUDE SQLCA	X	X	X			115
OPEN cursor-name	X	X	X		X	121

SELECT [DISTINCT] {expression1 [, expression2]...}
                              {*}
    [INTO   :host-variable1 [, :host-variable2] ...]
    FROM   table-name1 [alias1] [, table-name2 [alias2]]...
    [WHERE   search-condition]
	X	X	X		X	115

UPDATE table-name
    SET column-name1 = expression1
        [, column-name2 = expression2] ...
    WHERE CURRENT OF cursor-name
	X	X	X		X	129
						132

DATA TYPES						
CHAR(length)	X	X	X	X	X	14
CHARACTER(length)					X	
DATE	X	X	X	X		15
DECIMAL (p,s)	X	X			X	14
DOUBLE PRECISION	X				X	
FLOAT	X	X		X	X	14
INTEGER	X	X		X	X	14
LONG			X			
LONG VARCHAR	X	X				
MONEY				X		
NUMBER [(p,s)]			X			
NUMERIC [(p,s)]					X	
REAL					X	
SMALLINT	X	X		X	X	14
VARCHAR(length)	X	X				

	DB2	SQL/DS	ORACLE	XDB	ANSI Standard	Text Page

COMPARISON OPERATORS

	DB2	SQL/DS	ORACLE	XDB	ANSI Standard	Text Page
=	X	X	X	X	⁼ X	23
<	X	X	X	X	X	23
<=	X	X	X	X	X	23
>	X	X	X	X	X	23
>=	X	X	X	X	X	23
<>					X	23
!=			X	X		23
¬ =	X	X				23
BETWEEN	X	X	X	X	X	31
IN	X	X	X	X	X	32
LIKE	X	X	X	X	X	34
EXISTS	X	X		X	X	67
NULL	X	X	X	X	X	36
AND	X	X	X	X	X	25
OR	X	X	X	X	X	26
NOT	X	X	X	X	X	29
UNION	X	X		X		70

AGGREGATE FUNCTIONS

	DB2	SQL/DS	ORACLE	XDB	ANSI Standard	Text Page
AVG	X	X	X	X	X	47
COUNT	X	X	X	X	X	47
MAX	X	X	X	X	X	47
MIN	X	X	X	X	X	47
SUM	X	X	X	X	X	47
STDEV			X			
VARIANCE			X			
XSTDEV				X		
XVAR				X		

ARITHMETIC OPERATORS

	DB2	SQL/DS	ORACLE	XDB	ANSI Standard	Text Page
*	X	X	X	X	X	44
/	X	X	X	X	X	44
+	X	X	X	X	X	44
−	X	X	X	X	X	44

TABLE PRIVILEGES

	DB2	SQL/DS	ORACLE	XDB	ANSI Standard	Text Page
ALTER	X	X	X	X		93
DELETE	X	X	X	X	X	93
INDEX	X	X	X	X		93
INSERT	X	X	X	X	X	93
SELECT	X	X	X	X	X	93
UPDATE	X	X	X	X	X	93

	DB2	SQL/DS	ORACLE	XDB	ANSI Standard	Text Page
RULES FOR NAMING TABLES, VIEWS, COLUMNS, ETC.						
1. First character of name ...						
a. must begin with a letter.	x		x	x	x	13
b. may begin with an uppercase letter, $, #, or @. A name may begin with a digit (0–9) if it is enclosed in double quotes.		x				
2. Following the first character ...						
a. a name may contain uppercase letters, digits, or the underscore.	x				x	13
b. a name may contain uppercase letters, digits, the underscore, or the $ sign.			x			
c. a name may contain uppercase letters, the characters $, #, and @, digits, or the underscore.			x			
d. a name may contain letters, digits, or the characters #, $, %, &, {, }, and _ (underscore).				x		
LENGTH OF A TABLE, VIEW, OR INDEX NAME IS BETWEEN ...						
1. 1 to 18 characters.	x	x			x	13
2. 1 to 30 characters.			x			
3. 1 to 8 characters.				x		
LENGTH OF A COLUMN NAME IS BETWEEN ...						
1. 1 to 18 characters.	x	x			x	13
2. 1 to 30 characters.			x			
3. 1 to 15 characters.				x		

Answers to YOUR TURN Exercises

CHAPTER 2

1. a. CREATE TABLE STUDENT
```
( SID        CHAR(3)    NOT NULL,
  SNAME      CHAR(10),
  ...
```

b. CREATE TABLE STUDENT
```
( SID          CHAR(3)    NOT NULL,
  FIRST_NAME   CHAR(10),
  LAST_NAME    CHAR(15),
  ...
```

c. CREATE TABLE STUDENT
```
( SID        CHAR(3)    NOT NULL,
  SNAME      CHAR(10)   NOT NULL,
  ...
```

d. CREATE TABLE STUDENT
```
( SID        CHAR(3)    NOT NULL,
  SNAME      CHAR(10),
  SEX        CHAR(1),
  SAT        SMALLINT
  ...
```

e. CREATE TABLE STUDENT
```
( SID         CHAR(3)    NOT NULL,
  SNAME       CHAR(10),
  BIRTHDATE   CHAR(8),
  ...
```

2. CREATE TABLE COURSE
```
( FID       CHAR(3)    NOT NULL,
  FNAME     CHAR(10)   NOT NULL,
  EXT       CHAR(3),
  DEPT      CHAR(4),
  RANK      CHAR(4),
  SALARY    INTEGER )
```

3. CREATE TABLE CRSENRL
```
( CRSENRL  CHAR(6)    NOT NULL,
  SID      CHAR(3),
  GRADE    CHAR(1) )
```

4. DROP TABLE FACULTY

CHAPTER 3

1. SELECT SID, SNAME, SEX, MAJOR
  FROM   STUDENT

2. SELECT SNAME, GPA, MAJOR
  FROM   STUDENT

3. a. SELECT SNAME, MAJOR
   FROM   STUDENT
   WHERE SEX = 'F'

  b. SELECT SNAME, MAJOR
   FROM   STUDENT
   WHERE MAJOR != 'ACC'

4. SELECT *
  FROM   STUDENT
  WHERE GPA <= 2.5

5. SELECT SNAME, GPA
  FROM   STUDENT
  WHERE SEX = 'M' AND MAJOR = 'FIN'

6. SELECT SNAME, SEX, GPA
  FROM   STUDENT
  WHERE MAJOR = 'ACC' AND GPA >= 3.0

7. SELECT SNAME, MAJOR, GPA
  FROM   STUDENT
  WHERE MAJOR = 'MGT' OR MAJOR = 'ACC' OR GPA > 3.0

8. SELECT SNAME, MAJOR
  FROM   STUDENT
  WHERE SEX = 'F' AND (MAJOR = 'FIN' OR MAJOR = 'MKT')

9. SELECT SNAME, MAJOR, GPA
  FROM   STUDENT
  WHERE SEX = 'M' AND MAJOR = 'ACC' AND GPA > 2.5

10. SELECT SNAME, SEX, MAJOR, GPA
   FROM   STUDENT
   WHERE ((MAJOR = 'MKT' OR MAJOR = 'MGT') AND GPA > 3.5)
      OR (MAJOR = 'FIN' AND SEX = 'F')

11. SELECT SNAME
   FROM   STUDENT
   WHERE NOT (SEX = 'M')

12. SELECT SNAME, MAJOR
   FROM   STUDENT
   WHERE MAJOR = 'ACC' OR MAJOR = 'FIN'

13. SNAME

  PELNICK
  GAMBRELL
  ANDERSON

  AND is evaluated before OR; it is impossible to find a row that satisfies

   MAJOR = 'ACC' AND MAJOR = 'FIN'

  so essentially the query finds all GPA > 3.5.

14. SELECT   SNAME, GPA
     FROM   STUDENT
     WHERE   MAJOR = 'ACC' AND (GPA BETWEEN 2.9 AND 3.6)

15. SELECT   SNAME, MAJOR
     FROM   STUDENT
     WHERE   SEX = 'F' AND MAJOR IN ('ACC', 'FIN', 'MGT')

16. SELECT   SNAME
     FROM   STUDENT
     WHERE   SNAME LIKE '%R'

17. SELECT   SNAME
     FROM   STUDENT
     WHERE   SNAME LIKE 'S%R'

18. SELECT   SNAME
     FROM   STUDENT
     WHERE   SNAME LIKE '_ _ R%'

19. SELECT   SID, SNAME
     FROM   STUDENT
     ORDER BY SID

20. SELECT   SNAME, MAJOR, GPA
     FROM   STUDENT
     WHERE   GPA > 3.0
     ORDER BY MAJOR, GPA DESC

21. SELECT   SNAME, SEX
     FROM   STUDENT
     ORDER BY SEX, SNAME

CHAPTER 4

1. SELECT   FNAME, SALARY, SALARY * 1.05, ((SALARY * 1.05) – SALARY)
   FROM   FACULTY

2. SELECT   FNAME, SALARY/26
   FROM   FACULTY
   ORDER BY SALARY/26 DESC   or   ORDER BY 2 DESC

3. SELECT   FNAME
   FROM   FACULTY
   WHERE   SALARY/26 < 1000

4. SELECT   DEPT, SUM(SALARY)
   FROM   FACULTY
   GROUP BY DEPT

5. SELECT   MAX(SALARY)
   FROM   FACULTY

6. SELECT   RANK, AVG(SALARY), COUNT(*)
   FROM   FACULTY
   GROUP BY RANK

7. SELECT   RANK, AVG(SALARY), COUNT(*)
   FROM   FACULTY
   GROUP BY RANK
   ORDER BY AVG(SALARY)   or   ORDER BY 2 DESC

8. SELECT   SUM(SALARY)
   FROM   FACULTY
   WHERE   DEPT = 'ACC'

9. SELECT   DEPT, COUNT(*)
   FROM   FACULTY
   WHERE   RANK = 'ASSO'
   GROUP BY DEPT

10. SELECT   MAJOR, AVG(GPA)
    FROM   STUDENT
    GROUP BY MAJOR
    ORDER BY AVG(GPA)   or   ORDER BY 2 DESC

11. SELECT   MAJOR, AVG(GPA)
    FROM   STUDENT
    GROUP BY MAJOR
    HAVING   AVG(GPA) > 3.0

12. SELECT   MAJOR, COUNT(*)
    FROM   STUDENT
    GROUP BY MAJOR
    HAVING   COUNT(*) > 2

CHAPTER 5

1. | CRSNBR | CNAME |
| --- | --- |
| MKT610 | MKTING FOR MANAGERS |
| MKT670 | PRODUCT MARKETING |
| ACC610 | BASIC ACCOUNTING |

2. SELECT   STUDENT.SID, SNAME, CRSNBR, GRADE
   FROM   STUDENT, CRSENRL
   WHERE   STUDENT.SID = CRSENRL.SID
   ORDER BY STUDENT.SID

3. SELECT   STUDENT.SID, SNAME, COURSE.CRSNBR, CNAME, GRADE
   FROM   STUDENT, CRSENRL, COURSE
   WHERE   STUDENT.SID = CRSENRL.SID
     AND   CRSENRL.CRSNBR = COURSE.CRSNBR
   ORDER BY STUDENT.SID

4. SELECT   COURSE.CRSNBR, CNAME, SNAME
   FROM   COURSE, CRSENRL, FACULTY, STUDENT
   WHERE COURSE.CRSNBR = 'FIN601'
     AND   COURSE.CRSNBR = CRSENRL.CRSNBR
     AND   CRSENRL.SID = STUDENT.SID
     AND   FACULTY.FID = COURSE.FID

5. SELECT SNAME
   FROM   STUDENT
   WHERE SID IN

          (SELECT SID
            FROM   CRSENRL
            WHERE GRADE = 'A')

6. No. When the output includes columns from more than one table, a subquery cannot be used as the main query.

```
 7. SELECT    FNAME
    FROM      FACULTY
    WHERE     FID =
                        ( SELECT    FID
                          FROM      COURSE
                          WHERE     CRSNBR = 'FIN601' )

 8. SELECT    SNAME
    FROM      STUDENT
    WHERE     GPA =
                        ( SELECT    MAX (GPA)
                          FROM      STUDENT )

 9. SELECT    FNAME
    FROM      FACULTY
    WHERE     DEPT = 'ACC'
      AND     SALARY >
                        ( SELECT    SALARY
                          FROM      FACULTY
                          WHERE     FNAME = 'JARDIN' )

10. SELECT    SNAME, GPA
    FROM      STUDENT
    WHERE     GPA >
                        ( SELECT    AVG(GPA)
                          FROM      STUDENT )

11. SELECT       MAJOR, AVG(GPA)
    FROM         STUDENT
    GROUP BY     MAJOR
    HAVING       AVG(GPA) >
                            ( SELECT    AVG(GPA)
                              FROM      STUDENT )

12. SELECT    FNAME, DEPT, SALARY
    FROM      FACULTY
    WHERE     SALARY >
                        ( SELECT    AVG(SALARY)
                          FROM      FACULTY )

13. SELECT    FNAME
    FROM      FACULTY
    WHERE     SALARY =
                        ( SELECT    MAX(SALARY)
                          FROM      FACULTY )

14. SELECT    SNAME
    FROM      STUDENT, CRSENRL, COURSE
    WHERE     CNAME = 'INTRO TO MANAGEMENT'
      AND     COURSE.CRSNBR = CRSENRL.CRSNBR
      AND     GRADE = 'F'
      AND     CRSENRL.SID = STUDENT.SID

15. SELECT    FNAME, CRSNBR, CNAME
    FROM      FACULTY, COURSE
    WHERE     FACULTY.FID = COURSE.FID
      AND     COURSE.FID IN
                        ( SELECT      FID
                          FROM        COURSE
                          GROUP BY    FID
                          HAVING      COUNT(*) > 1)
```

CHAPTER 6

1. INSERT INTO COURSE
VALUES('FIN603','PORTFOLIO MANAGEMENT',4,25,'138')

2. INSERT INTO CRSENRL(CRSNBR,SID)
VALUES('FIN601','506')

3. CREATE TABLE TRNSCRPT
```
( CRSNBR     CHAR(6)     NOT NULL,
  SID        CHAR(3)     NOT NULL,
  GRADE      CHAR(1),
  TERM       CHAR(3) )
```

INSERT INTO TRNSCRPT(CRSNBR,SID,GRADE)
SELECT   CRSNBR, SID, GRADE
FROM   CRSENRL

4. DELETE FROM STUDENT
WHERE SNAME = 'FAGIN'

All courses in the CRSENRL table that FAGIN is enrolled in should be deleted.

5. UPDATE STUDENT
SET   MAJOR = 'MKT'
WHERE   SID = '218'

6. UPDATE COURSE
SET   CNAME = 'INVESTMENT ANALYSIS'
         MAXENRL = 40
WHERE   CRSNBR = 'FIN602'

7. UPDATE FACULTY
SET   SALARY = SALARY * 1.07
WHERE   DEPT = 'ACC' OR DEPT = 'FIN'

CHAPTER 7

1. FID   FNAME   EXT

098   KENNEDY   176
151   DARDEN   250

2. CREATE VIEW ROSTER(CRSNBR,CRSNAME,FACNAME,STUID,STUNAME)

The rest of the code is the same.

3. CREATE VIEW SCHEDULE
AS SELECT   CRSNBR, CNAME, CREDIT, MAXENRL, COURSE.FID, FNAME
    FROM   COURSE, FACULTY
    WHERE   COURSE.FID = FACULTY.FID

4. SELECT   CRSNBR, CNAME
FROM   SCHEDULE
WHERE   FNAME = 'KENNEDY'

5. An error occurs. You can access only grouped data using this view.

CHAPTER 8

1. GRANT   SELECT
ON   STUDENT, CRSENRL
TO   PRES

2. CREATE VIEW CLERKVW
    AS   SELECT   FID, FNAME, EXT, DEPT, RANK
        FROM   FACULTY

  GRANT   SELECT
  ON   CLERKVW
  TO   CLERK

3. GRANT   UPDATE
  ON   STUDENT
  TO   ARDEN, FRANCO

4. GRANT   ALL
  ON   COURSE
  TO   PUBLIC

5. REVOKE   ALL
  ON   COURSE
  FROM   PUBLIC

CHAPTER 9

1. SELECT   *
  FROM   SYSCOLS

2. SELECT   TNAME
  FROM   SYSTABLE
  WHERE   TNAME = 'V'

3. ALTER   TABLE FACULTY
  ADD   DATE_HRD CHAR(8)   or   ADD DATE_HRD DATE

4. CREATE TABLE CRSENRL2
    (CRSNBR   CHAR(6)   NOT NULL,
      SID   CHAR(3)   NOT NULL,
      GRADE   CHAR(2))

  INSERT INTO CRSENRL2
    SELECT   *
    FROM   CRSENRL

5. SYSTABLE
    CRSENRL2 T
  SYSCOLS

TBNAME	NAME	COLTYPE	LENGTH	COLNO
STUDENT	DATE_HRD	CHAR	8	7
CRSENRL2	CRSNBR	CHAR	6	1
CRSENRL2	SID	CHAR	3	2
CRSENRL2	GRADE	CHAR	2	3

6. CREATE UNIQUE INDEX CRENRINDX
  ON CRSENRL
    (CRSNBR, SID)

CHAPTER 10

1. B030-OUTPUT.
    IF SQLCODE = 0
       MOVE HGPA TO OUTGPA
       DISPLAY ' '.
       DISPLAY 'Sex   :', HSEX
       DISPLAY 'Major :', HMAJOR
       DISPLAY 'GPA   :', OUTGPA
    ELSE IF SQLCODE = 100
       DISPLAY ' No Student Found for This ID '
    ELSE
       PERFORM C010-ERROR.

2. a. DISPLAY 'Enter Desired Major'.
    ACCEPT HMAJOR.

    b.   EXEC SQL
       INCLUDE SQLCA
    END EXEC.

       EXEC SQL BEGIN DECLARE SECTION END-EXEC.
    01 HSID   PIC XXX.
    01 HGRADE   PIC 9V99.
    01 HCRSNBR PIC X.
    EXEC SQL END DECLARE SECTION END-EXEC.

3. The host variable HSID has no value when the OPEN statement is executed. Thus, the active set of the cursor structure cannot be defined.

4. a. 01 HSID   PIC XXX.
       01 HGRADE   PIC 9V99.
       01 HCRSNBR PIC X(6).

    b. DECLARE STU_CLASS_ROSTER CURSOR FOR
       SELECT SID, SNAME, GRADE
       FROM   CRSENRL, STUDENT
       WHERE   CRSNBR = :HCRSNBR
         AND   CRSENRL.SID = STUDENT.SID
       FOR UPDATE OF GRADE

APPENDIX A

1. a. COLUMN   CRSNBR   HEADING   'COURSE NUMBER'
       COLUMN   CNAME   HEADING   'COURSE TITLE'

    b. COLUMN   SNAME   HEADING   'STUDENT | NAME'
       COLUMN   MAJOR   HEADING   'I | MAJOR'
       COLUMN   GPA   HEADING   'GRADE | POINT | AVERAGE'

Sample Tables for Student Record System

STUDENT Table

SID	SNAME	SEX	MAJOR	GPA
987	POIRIER	F	MGT	3.2
763	PARKER	F	FIN	2.7
218	RICHARDS	M	ACC	2.4
359	PELNICK	F	FIN	3.6
862	FAGIN	M	MGT	2.2
748	MEGLIN	M	MGT	2.8
506	LEE	M	FIN	2.7
581	GAMBRELL	F	MKT	3.8
372	QUICK	F	MGT	3.5
126	ANDERSON	M	ACC	3.7

FACULTY Table

FID	FNAME	EXT	DEPT	RANK	SALARY
036	BARGES	325	MGT	ASSO	35000
117	JARDIN	212	FIN	FULL	33000
098	KENNEDY	176	ACC	ASSO	30000
075	SAMPLE	171	MKT	ASST	25000
138	WARD	125	MGT	INST	20000
219	PETERS	220	FIN	FULL	45000
151	DARDEN	250	ACC	ASSO	37000
113	PIERCE	205	MGT	INST	22000

CRSENRL Table

CRSNBR	SID	GRADE
MGT630	987	A
FIN602	987	B
MKT610	987	A
FIN601	763	B
FIN602	763	B
ACC610	763	B
ACC610	218	A
ACC661	218	A
MGT630	218	C
MGT630	359	F
MGT681	359	B
MKT610	359	A
MKT610	862	A
MKT670	862	A
ACC610	862	B
MGT630	748	C
MGT681	748	B
FIN601	748	A

COURSE Table

CRSNBR	CNAME	CREDIT	MAXENRL	FID
MGT630	INTRO TO MANAGEMENT	4	30	138
FIN601	MANAGERIAL FINANCE	4	25	117
MKT610	MKTING FOR MANAGERS	3	35	075
ACC661	TAXATION	3	30	098
FIN602	INVESTMENT SKILLS	3	25	219
ACC610	BASIC ACCOUNTING	4	25	098
MGT681	INTERNATIONAL MGT	3	20	036
MKT670	PRODUCT MARKETING	3	20	075

Index

SAVE $100.00 ON XDB-SQL

XDB-STUDENT (a limited version of XDB-SQL) is free to adopters of *A Primer on SQL*.

If you wish to purchase XDB-SQL, return this coupon with your order and save $100.00 off the price of the unlimited commercial version of XDB-SQL.*

PLEASE SEND ME THE FOLLOWING SOFTWARE:

Number	Product		Price	Ordering Total
_____	XDB-SQL	(Database manager, interactive SQL, report writer, and other tools)		
		Regular price	$ 495.00 ea.	
		Price with coupon	$ 395.00 ea.	$_____
_____	XDB-FORMS	(Forms manager)	$ 295.00 ea.	$_____
_____	XDB-LEARN	(Limited-use version of XDB-SQL and XDB-FORMS)	$ 29.00 ea.	$_____
_____	XDB-C	(Programming Interface for Microsoft C)	$ 295.00 ea.	$_____
			SUBTOTAL	$_____
		Maryland residents add 5% sales tax		$_____
		Shipping and handling		$_____10.00_____
			TOTAL	$_____

PAYMENT METHOD

Check _____ Money Order _____ VISA _____ MASTERCARD _____

Card number _____ Expires _____

Signature _____

Name _____

Company/Institution _____

Address _____

City, State, Zip _____

For more information on XDB-COBOL, XDB-UNIX, and other XDB Products, call (301)779-5486.

* This offer not valid with any other offer. One coupon per customer please. Prices are subject to change without notice. This offer expires December 31, 1988.